Etchings 35.1

Literary and Fine Arts Magazine of the
University of Indianapolis
Fall 2022

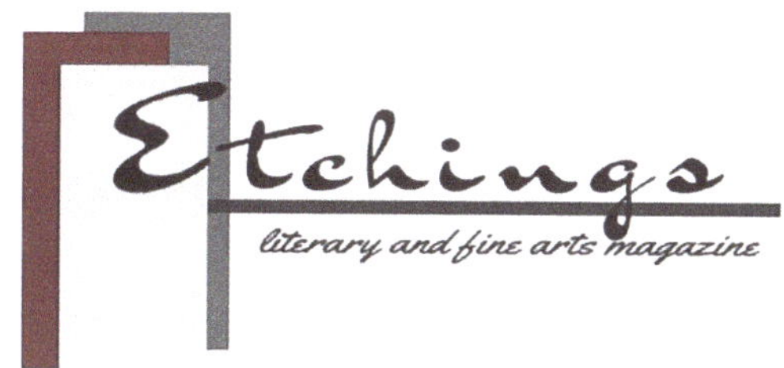

1400 E. Hanna Ave.
Indianapolis, IN 46227

Cover Design by Etchings Staff
Cover Art by Kiara Dottery
Printed by IngramSpark
ingramspark.com

Editorial Staff

Submissions Editor

Emma Knaack

Managing Editor

Alrielle Viewegh

Design Editors

Desteni Guidry
Breanna Emmett

Communications Coordinator

Mackenzie Hyatt

Social Media Coordinators

Sophia Atkinson
Ethan Thurston

Editors

Jawaher Alkhalifa
Liza Harris
Sam Jackson
Alex Phillips-Hedge

Faculty Advisor

Liz Whiteacre

Table of Contents

***CW is short for Content warning. Please read and review these pieces with caution.**

Letter from the Staff

Dear Readers,

We want to thank you for taking the time to engage with our magazine. It includes wonderful works of art, prose, and poetry that illuminate a variety of issues, feelings, and scenes. In addition to these works, we also have included an interview with poet and former faculty advisor Elizabeth Weber, judge of this issue's Dorlis Gott Armentrout Award.

This edition is special because it is our 35th anniversary edition. In total, this culminates in forty-three editions of *Etchings*. *Etchings* has deep roots; it was originally born from its predecessor *Tusitala*, a literary magazine from when the University of Indianapolis was Indiana Central University. The rebirth of this magazine resulted in the Dorlis Gott Armentrout Award, which honors Dr. Robert Brooker's sister-in-law. This issue is a celebration of the creative arts and its history at UIndy.

Please keep in mind that our works are diverse and not suitable to all audiences, so some pieces have content warnings. They will be marked with yellow on the edge of the first page of the poem or story and have the specific reason for the warning below the title and author's name. These works, while of quality, might trigger people for various reasons. In our ever-changing world, we need to be mindful of as many groups as we can and provide transparency in our magazine in order to celebrate and promote inclusivity.

We appreciate the work done by our staff and, especially, from Professor Liz Whiteacre, our faculty advisor, for helping us through the complex process of creating a magazine. *Etchings*' staff this year was large, which has given us the opportunity to amplify more voices, hear differing opinions, and create a magazine that we believe represents many facets of our campus, community, and current issues. Together, we have created a magazine that we hope highlights diverse voices as we celebrate this anniversary edition of the magazine.

If you have any interest in being a part of the second issue of our 35th anniversary, please see our call for submissions at the back of this issue. Students may join the one credit hour class, ENGL 379: Etchings Magazine, and be part of 35.2's staff.

Thank you for your interest in our work and the work of the UIndy community.

Etchings Magazine Staff, Fall 2022

2022 Roberta Lee Brooker Fiction Award

Unkempt

by Z Wilkinson

The matted grey tabby stretches in her spot on the bed, previously nestled up by the pillow into a tight, warm ball. She licks her paws, tail swinging around to hug her thigh, brushing up against the full bottle of Zoloft on the bedside table, perched beside an open bottle of water, the cap lost to the darkness under the bed; a fun toy. Stepping down onto the tough, carpeted floor, she strides over to the window, placing her soft white paws onto the sill to lean up and take a look. The thick blackout curtains move to scatter crisp afternoon sunlight across the foot of the bed when she noses them, peeking out at the unkempt, feebly-fenced backyard. She spots a banditry of black-capped chickadees yanking worms from the mushy, cold dirt, interrupted by thin patches of tall yellow grass.

Her eyes dart watching for a few minutes before her routine continues, and she prowls from the bedroom, door open, inviting her into a dimly lit hallway, the walls free of paintings and photographs and decoration, a dirty yellow. She stops at her dish to drink, stepping between shards of glass clustered on the tile, the automatic jug bubbling and gulping as she relieves it of the last of its water. She paws at the opening in the hopes she'll discover more, but gives up quickly. She leaves a wet paw print as she steps through unpaid bills scattered below the kitchen counter, knocked over days ago. The cat shimmies her shoulders before leaping onto the scuffed granite counter, treading lightly through the overflowing sink, nose flaring at the smell of soggy, days old, rotting vegetables. She peeks out of the window there now, watching a squirrel dart up the thick, short tree squatting in the near-center of the back yard, ears pointing forward and pupils dilating. Her concentration is broken as she steps down from the windowsill to itch, frayed faux leather collar jangling in protest as it swings around her thin neck. She lets out a silent yawn, teeth baring, before hopping down to the linoleum once again, slowly walking to the living room to investigate the couch.

A thick, heavy blanket lays clinging to its arm, draped onto the floor, and she moves past it to shove her face in between the cushions, sniffing, before popping back out, a scuba diver coming up for air. Everything smells of dust and sugar, and she often finds bits of pastries she isn't allowed to have nestled into the crevices of the furniture. A branch of the stumpy tree outside smacks against the back window and she jumps, head just snapping up to meet its pitch black gaze, staring over the back of the dark brown, synthetic fiber couch. The curtain doesn't move, and she decides it isn't worth checking, moving past the low wooden table which seems too far from the couch to be good for anything. She reaches the tower in the corner in mere seconds, stretching out her back as she leans against the tall, torn pole, claws greeting the fibers and ripping them apart. Then she digs in, climbing to the very top, where she could bump her head against the ceiling, to look out across the house, in awe of her kingdom. She suddenly twists to scratch at her neck with her back foot.

It's dark inside, as always, but she can see well, nearly blinded when she peeks outside. An emaciated light echoes from the kitchen to the front of the house; one window is missing a curtain, the other with an uncovered sliver playing at the edge of the sill, casting a thin rod of light onto the grainy, dirty rug sheltering the doorway. Skinny sneakers and lace-up boots decorate the patch of hardwood there, strings squashed and stretched and fun to bite. The cat settles to nap, perched atop the highest platform which is covered in a coarse off-white fluff.

The cat is awoken by the sound of the door knob jiggling. There is a quiet, metallic click as the lock turns, then the door swings open cautiously, setting off a fast, high-pitched "bee-bee-bee-beep" somewhere in the house. The cat watches, intrigued, as a short man walks inside. He looks around before making eye contact with her, and she stares back at him. One of his eyes is a milky white; his hair falls in between his eyes and remains short on the sides.

"— Misty," she hears, leaping down from the top of the tower, legs straining under the sudden pressure at her ankles. She stretches, front half pressed against the floor, back end raised before meowing at the man and striding over to him. She rubs against his ankles, which are covered in a rough, damp pair of dark-wash jeans; his shoes smell like rain and salt. The sound of him is warm. He pushes the door shut again. "— eat? ——— hungry," the cat hears, showing off with a slow spin before letting out a loud, guttural meow. He makes a sound one could only describe as a chatter, setting down his hefty bag and walking to the kitchen. His shoes leave faint marks on the carpet, then the tile, squeaking. The cat follows him, sitting prettily in front of her empty food bowl. It's small, a color somewhere between grey and orange, a light plastic. She sniffs at it, her tags clinking softly against its edge.

The man inspects her water dish, tearing its top from its bottom and bringing it to the sink to refill–he makes a sound, and then comes the loud clatter of dishes as he moves them to the countertop to make space. Water spills down over the counter's edge, murky and brown. The cat lets out another hungry meow, standing and walking over to the man to paw at his legs.

"—— food, Misty, —. Mommy ——— hm?" She meows again in response, watching him return to her water, replacing the jug, which spurts and grumbles as it spits into the dish. She takes a long drink, before being distracted by the sounds of kibble. The man pours some into her shallow bowl, pushing the pile of bills aside with his foot. She settles in to eat, voraciously, taking large bites and chewing too quickly. Her collar jangles at her neck, smacking at the plastic; her ears turn away from the sound. A loud breath comes from the man as he exits the room–she glances up from her gorging to watch him walk down the hall, licking her lips before finishing her meal. It sits heavy in her stomach. She sits up once the bowl is empty, licking her paws and stepping over to her water bowl. She dips a paw in, shaking her leg in self-protest, before licking in between her pads. Her attention jerks to the hallway before her ritual can finish, two pairs of footsteps getting closer. She stills.

"— okay, — fed —, —— Moku. Move, Misty."

The cat side-steps as the two approach, the man and woman. He's holding her hand and they walk into the kitchen, glass crunching under his shoe; he recoils and steps around it, pulling the woman out of the way. The cat sits, tail caressing her leg, paws tight against each other, shoulders scrunched, neck stretched. A fluorescent bulb overhead unsteadily flickers to life, bringing the room from the dim glow of the afternoon to a sickly white.

The man opens a grimey cupboard below the sink, its hinges squeaking, dishwater staining the door, to grab a small dustpan and handheld broom. "Moku ——— okay?" He sweeps up the shards; they glitter, crackling and hissing at each other as they're moved.

"—— Misty —— wet food?" The cat's gaze snaps up to the woman's face and she meows, raspy. The woman's eyes are covered by a black band; it wraps around her head, frayed ends tied at the back. Her skin is bright pink in some places and pale in others, looking wet.

"—— wet food?" After the man repeats the sound, the woman nods, gesturing vaguely to a certain cupboard. The cat leaps onto the countertop, tail swaying, watching as he grabs a familiar-looking can and cracks it open, a deeper sound, like paper tearing. Her eyes dilate. The man chatters, picking up her once-again-empty bowl and spooning the wet food into it, mashing it down. She waits impatiently, jumping down from the counter and returning to her seat on the floor, shaking her ears. She eats much more slowly this time, the thick smell of salmon invading her nose.

The tile below her holds countless dust mites and dead gnats–a lifeless spider lays upside down within the counter's toe space, limbs tangled and locked together after a ferocious one-sided battle. The cat pauses, her stomach turning, still unable to catch up, and she looks at the two standing above her. They're making sounds at each other while the man tackles the mountain of cookware in the sink, and the woman's closed into herself, arms locked and legs turned inward. The cat walks over to her, rubbing against her leg and meowing quietly. The woman stoops to pick her up by the abdomen, quickly moving her hand to support her bottom, hefting her over one shoulder. The cat bumps her head against the woman's ear, purring softly into the fluffy neckline of her cardigan.

"Misty —— Moku, —." The man's voice is soft. The woman pets the cat gently, scratching her just behind the ear and then tensing, recoiling, holding her out to the man.

"Riley — " He scrambles to turn off the sink and dry his hands before taking her. The woman begins to sound frightened, backing away until she's against the counter, grabbing its rounded edge.

The cat squirms in the man's damp arms and he sets her down on the floor. She stares up at them for a moment before strolling down the hallway. Hair piles up against the baseboards and weaves itself into the fibers of the carpet. She walks into the bedroom, stopping to sniff at the air–a dustiness permeates the room, unsettled by the opening of the curtain. It's much brighter now, light strangling the rumped bedspread, blankets disturbed and half-draping over the edge of the bed. The bedside water bottle is full of condensation, old and warm, the texture of spit. The cat crouches down to crawl underneath the bed, breath quickening, setting her sights on the bottle cap. She jumps forward to pick it up in her mouth, meowing, a quiet and almost speech-like sound. "He-wowr?" she repeats, clasping the cap between her teeth and crawling back out. She drops it, bats it away, jumps for it again. This continues.

She smacks it against a glass frame leaned against the wall beside the window, the image inside covered in layers and layers of inharmoniously different colors of paint. The glass is dusty. There's a "plink" where the bottle cap smacks against it, while the cat keeps trying to pick it up again. The room grows brighter as a cloud passes away from the sun, illuminating further the ugliness of the walls, the floors, the corners. The cat stops, staring down at the cap that lies a foot away from her. She crouches low, ears pressed back against her skull–not much between it, and her fur–before pouncing, smacking it further away and pouncing again. Her strange meowing starts again when she finally secures the cap in her mouth.

She jumps onto the bed with it, shaking her head before letting go. It lands on the table with a soft thud, cushioned by a stack of papers, a folder squashed under the weight of them. A pill bottle rattles as the cat knocks it over, pushing her way through the mess to smack the cap onto the floor. In her haste, the water bottle falls too, spilling tremendously onto the carpet, and onto her. She hisses, startled, leaping away, shaking and twitching before bolting out of the room and zipping onto the couch. Her claws dig into the fabric and she shakes again, tail puffing out as she rips her way across the carpet and up the tower. She has both the man and woman's attention, though the woman is looking elsewhere.

"Misty? ———, Moku, ——." The man sneezes out a

breath, leaving to walk into the bedroom. The cat shakes atop the tower, furiously licking her fur. Her claws scratch at her tongue and curl in on themselves as she cleans her paws. "Misty..." The woman walks over to the tower, pressing a hand against its midsection and pushing it up the pole until it reaches the cat's perch. She feels around a little before making contact with fur, petting the cat and feeling the wetness.

The cat looks down at her, shaking subtly in her dampness. Up close the cat can see all the defects in the woman's skin. Her face is marred with dark patches of waxy pink scabs, healing burns striking through her cheeks and worming underneath the cloth shielding her eyes. There are thin sacs of fluid that have just popped lining her jaw, ear, hairline, broken up by strips of raw flesh trailing down her neck. The backs of her hands, too, are rough and pink. Her skin is uneven and bumpy, and the cat has long since forgotten the startling image of dark recesses taking place of the woman's eyes. She does not remember tipping over a tall glass of water, allowing two bright white orbs to roll out, decorated only by a small circle of hazel, becoming her next plaything until they were lost to the dim, sunken corners of the bedroom floor.

The woman stops touching her, head turning in the direction of the hallway, the man is making sounds back there. The woman leaves to follow him, fingers tracing the way and leaving a wet line that quickly fades. The cat continues to lick herself, desperate to remove the water. She tastes dirt, and her skin gives way to the depressions between her ribs. Her tongue catches on the hair, pulling at it.

The woman walks slowly back into the bedroom, stilling in the middle of the hallway, leaning against the wall at her side and crumbling to the floor. She starts sniffling, making quiet noises. The cat is too preoccupied with her own stress to be concerned with jumping down from her perch and rushing over to comfort her like usual. The man soon comes to her aid, crouching down beside her and making a warning sound before gently grabbing her arms and pulling her into his embrace.

The cat decides she isn't getting any dryer. She starts rolling around on the perch, squirming her back against the rough fabric and meowing quietly. She does a long stretch, rolling back onto her stomach and surveying the living room. There are mouse droppings scattered just underneath the couch, beside the back door, shoved up against the corners of the room. Though, there aren't any mice. Bugs which came in to escape the start of a cold winter lay infrequently smushed into the carpet. The woman makes a loud noise and it startles the cat, her head snapping to look down the hallway, body lowering further into the perch. Her hands are tangled into her hair, long and thin over her shoulders, not doing much to shield her face. Her stubby fingernails are stained with dry blood. The man moves away from her a little, before slowly placing his hands on her shoulders and making a noise.

The woman seems to go limp, head sagging onto her knees which are pulled to her chest, wrists slack around her ankles. The house is silent. The cat stares, wide-eyed, heart racing, beating angrily against her feeble ribcage.

"—— vet, Riley?"

"————. —— okay?"

"No. Misty ———." The woman starts sounding scared again. The cat makes herself even smaller, invisible at the top of the perch, body covered by its hard underside.

" —— vet. —— eat—, —— feed ——."

"Okay."

The cat waits until it feels safe to come down, slowly climbing down her tower and hiding behind it for a moment once she's firmly on the ground. She peeks around the scratching pole, watching the man walk towards her. He crouches down and she stands up, stepping out to greet him with her snout against his outstretched hand. He scratches behind her ear and his eyes get thinner; he gently pats her back. She lets out a high-pitched meow, nuzzling his arm. He gives a loud, long breath, sitting down and crossing his legs. She moves into his lap, flopping against his stomach and stretching her legs. They're thin, paws beginning to look too big attached to them, and her stomach would be concave if not for her primordial pouch. Her head holds onto most of her fat.

"——— bath, Misty." (Missy?). The cat stills hearing this sound, before curling around on her back and looking up at him with pleading eyes. "—— cute, —— bath —." He gently scoops her up into a more carry-able position, a hand around her waist, another under her, and stands.

The bathroom feels damp, as if the shower has been on. There's toothpaste, splashes of rubbing alcohol, scraps of band-aid wrappers, and snippets of gauze all over the sink; flecks of long-dried blood pepper the off-white surface. The man closes the door and sets the cat down as they enter. The rug beneath her paws is soft, the fibers a short and fuzzy cotton. She opens and closes her paws, before remembering the sound the man had made before. She looks at the tub–there is no shower curtain. Instead, the occasional metal bar is screwed haphazardly into the wall, chipping the light blue paint around it. The shower tiles are covered in soap scum. There are several half-empty bottles of product scattered around the shower shelves, on the rim of the tub, in the trash can. Some of them are for washing, others for sanitizing; for wounds, for skin, for surfaces.

The man sheds his jacket and drapes it against the shelf. He walks over to the tub, closing then sitting on the toilet beside it and turning on the faucet. The knob makes a terrible creak. The cat crouches down on the rug, curling up into a tight loaf, watching him. He looks around, pawing through the open shelves of the small cabinet pressed between the wall and door, then opening the cupboard below the sink. He grabs a tall bottle there, setting it on the rim of the tub and running his wrist under the water, turning the knobs, waiting, then turning them off.

"Okay, Misty." The man leans over and picks her up–her claws stick in the rug and pull it up with her until she loses her grip and it falls, crumpled, back onto the floor. He holds her in his lap for a moment, removing her collar and setting it on the sink, before shifting to the rim of the tub and gently lowering her in. There are only a few inches of water, and she stands there, paralyzed by discomfort. He keeps a hand pressed into her back, grabbing an empty cup from the floor beside the toilet. Slowly, he scoops up some water and runs it over her back and neck. The cat squirms but stays standing, ears flattening against her skull.

"—— Misty… —— good girl…" The man holds her neck scruff with one hand, opening the bottle he had grabbed prior with the other, and dumping a hefty amount onto her back. She starts meowing; a strange, frog-in-the-throat sound. The man makes a soft hissing sound in response, starting to rub the liquid into her fur. He seems to start, making a quiet noise. The water below her is tinged with a thin wisp of red, swirling around her legs. "———— fleas, Misty…" He moves his hand to grab her head and pull her ear to the side, peering his head closer to her. She squirms more, lifting a paw to push at him. "————— vet, huh, girl." The man's voice gets quieter.

He turns her around and picks up either of her back legs, craning his neck. Her heart races in her chest and she continues to cry out. The man makes another soft hiss. He returns his attention to rubbing her, scratching at her skin, momentarily easing an itch she has failed to curb. Soon he is dumping water over her again, trying with his hand to shield her face from the onslaught. The cat shivers where she stands, placing her paws on the rim of the tub and straining every muscle against the man's grip on her scruff to achieve her escape. The water starts draining from the tub and the man grabs a towel from a nearby shelf, scooping her into his arms wrapped within it. The cat sneezes, wanting nothing more than to bolt from the room. He dries her, a long few minutes in which the cat desperately tries to claw her way through the door. He clips her collar back onto her, rubbing the cheap fabric between his fingers before opening the door.

The cat shoves her head through the open crack, pushing out into the hallway and bolting to and up the tower. Now, she must spend a long time cleaning herself. Her hair and bones stick out in all directions, eyes almost bulging from her skull, fur no longer working to hide the shape of her. The man returns, sitting beside the woman on the crumb-infested couch. He keeps to himself; the woman is collapsed into the seat, the hefty blanket swaddling her torso.

"Misty — fleas, Moku, ——— vet." The man's breath falls out of him. The woman does not say anything, her face covered by the blanket, knees pressed together, posture even more slouched than before. There is a small bird hopping in front of the window with no curtain, pecking at crumbs or twigs or bugs wedged into the cracks of the pavement. It pecks at the concrete with little success–all of the wild berries outside are dying, and all that's left are worms and aphids. The bird turns its head to look up and into the glass, and the cat has completely stopped what she was doing to stare back. She lowers her head further, pupils swallowing the swampy green of her eyes. The bird suddenly flies away, and the cat's head snaps to look at the man, who's standing up from the couch and gently grabbing the woman's hand.

"No. —— store, ——? ——— flea —." The woman pulls her hand away weakly.

"—— me, —."

"Okay," comes the woman's response, after a moment.

The two of them leave the living room and walk down the hallway, abandoning the blanket now strewn halfway across the floor. The cat jumps down from the tower and flops onto it immediately, pulling what was left atop the couch cushion onto her, rolling and scratching her wet skin against the fabric. She stretches her limbs before rolling back onto them, lowering her front to the ground as her back moves upward. She pads over to the water bowl silently and drinks. She can hear drawers being opened in the woman's room, then the closet door. It screams.

She walks over to the kitchen counter and leaps onto it, sitting in front of the window to soak in a final moment of sunlight from the backyard. The birds have left the grass, retiring to the stumpy tree beside the fence, one of its large branches laid across the ground, slowly leaving a dent in the dirt. One lone chickadee roams the fence, hopping away. The cat watches calmly, neck stretched upward to get a better look.

The cat hears footsteps and turns toward the hallway–the man waves a hand at her–and she jumps from the counter onto the floor, still-wet tail waving to greet him. He crouches and scratches behind her ears, rubbing under her chin.

"— back, ——— store —— flea —, okay? — good, Misty." His voice is quiet. He stands up again as the woman emerges from the hallway, hand pressed flat against the wall. It's almost impossible to see any of her skin now. The two of them walk to the front door and the cat follows, watching as the man opens the door–there comes the beeping sound, again–tugging the woman through. "—— Misty." The man follows her and closes it behind him. The knob jiggles as the lock clicks into place. The cat presses her paws against the door and meows quietly, then quickly moving to the front window and shoving the curtain aside to look. The man helps the woman climb into a small, dark blue car, which roars and hums once they're both inside. The cat meows again, a bit louder.

She stands at the window until her back legs tire, moving to sit a few feet in front of the door. She curls up into a tight ball, ears alert. She stares at the closed, scuffed front door until she grows tired from the day's excitement, and her eyes squint closed, settling to shiver there on the floor.

Illustrations for Fiction Award

These are solicited illustrations, selected by the *Etchings* staff, from work submitted by Art & Design Photography students.

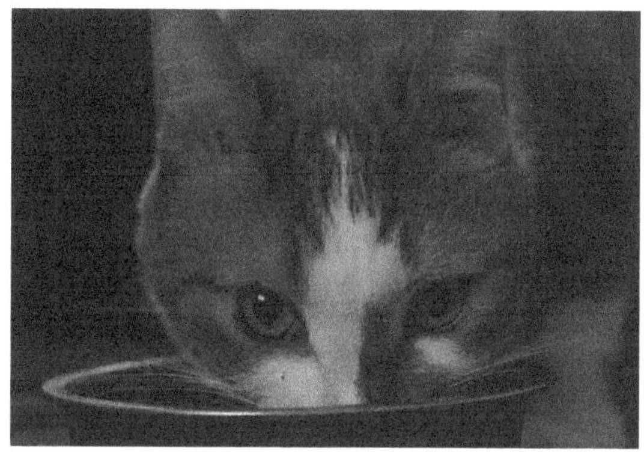

Eyes Darting,
Allison Burgess

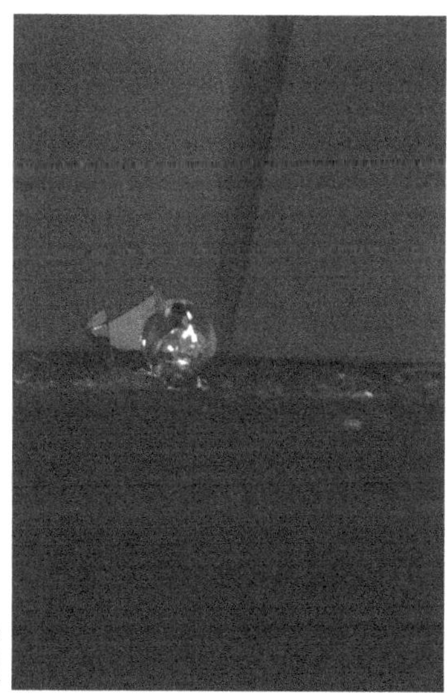

Fragile State of Mind,
AlyssaTodd

2022 Lucy Munro Brooker Poetry Prize

Language of Sin

by Tylyn K. Johnson

Did the Tower of Babel ever really fall?
That very structure that connected Heaven and Earth by a single tongue, how could it have fallen
when we can still speak through the feelings and vibrations of m u s i c which
caresses our skin with its rhythms
and holds us in its beautiful, illustrious sounds.
To speak in music is to allow a spiritual thing to wind its way in and out of our throats, to taste another person's fire and enjoy it.
Music, when it is in the air, grips onto us just as thorns hang onto a rose.

The story goes that god scattered the language of the people along the breeze, to eternity in condemnation of humans who would dare rise to a higher plane, but the people of Babel showed how they can fold the world before them when they sought to become the bridge between the corporeal and the ethereal. Their legacy is cemented for they kept their native tongue alive
by the sonic waves that dance across each and every breeze.
For their language was not so simple as speech, but of song, something without title that even the heavens became jealous of.
I mean, who of heaven's choirs could dare to match the exquisiteness of a songstress breathing beneath the whispers of the moon,
or even the melodies that we have crafted from a creek running clear?

And now here we are, expressing how carnal and earthly we be in so many more tongues, oh the
flames in these words could tear many
a city asunder

with a power that even the heavens lack against
Hell itself.
But such an affront to a god itself could only be made by
human lips, with these succulent, intemperate words coil
well around our fingers, a melody we've even turned divine
punishment into the soundtrack of pleasure. Of course, all
these words,
given life from all these tongues,
are made even more wicked by how they form songs that dance be-
tween us. So if the bricks of Babel have truly fallen,
then they have become the foundation of many unholy re-
frains, tasting ever-so-delightful.

Illustration for Poetry Prize

This is a solicited illustration, selected by the *Etchings* staff, from work submitted by Art & Design Photography students.

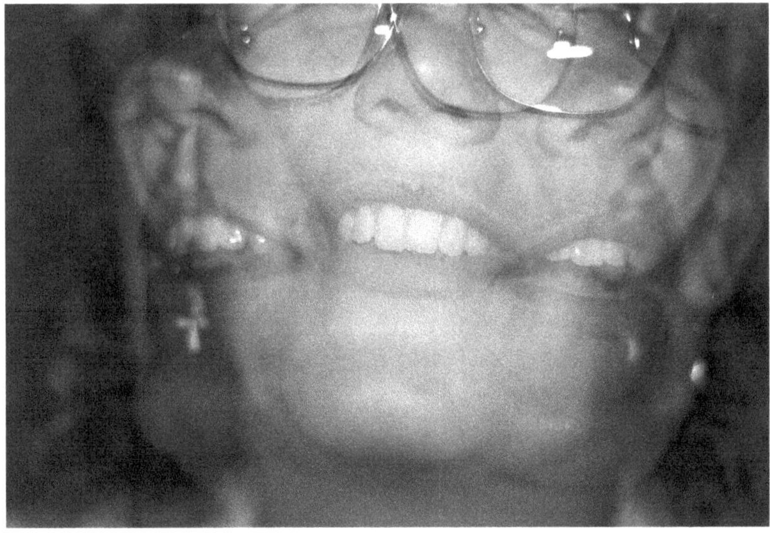

Of Many Tounges, Gabriel Eastridge

Anna Elizabeth Gott Memorial Art Awards

The recipients of the **UIndy Anna Elizabeth Gott Memorial Art Award** were **Isabelle Phelps** and **Lauren Railer.** This award, honoring outstanding senior Art & Design majors, was endowed as a memorial in 1978 by Anna's sister, Mary E. Gott. Anna Elizabeth Gott had traveled widely in her career with the federal government and, in doing so, developed a deep interest in the great masterpieces of world art. This contest was judged by Art & Design faculty.

Mary E. Gott Award for Excellence in Art

The recipients of the **UIndy Mary E. Gott Award** for **Excellence in Art** were **Savannah Muschong** and **Jes Brockman Artemiev**. This award, honoring outstanding junior Art & Design majors, was endowed in 1984 by UIndy Professor Emeritus Robert Brooker and his wife, Ruth, as a tribute to Mrs. Brooker's aunt, Mary E. Gott. Mary, like her sister Anna, held a government post in Washington, D.C. and loved art. This contest was judged by Art & Design faculty.

2022 Art Awards Best of Show: Studio

Ambivalent by Cameron Owens

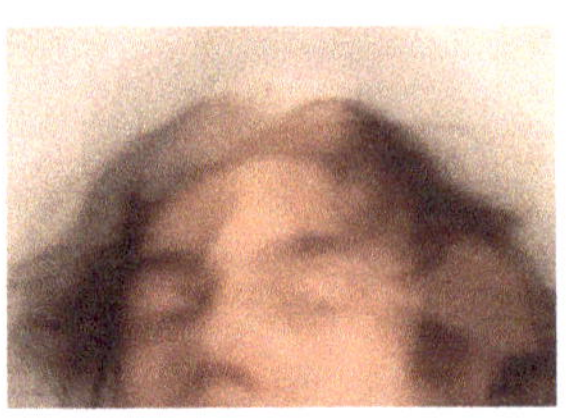

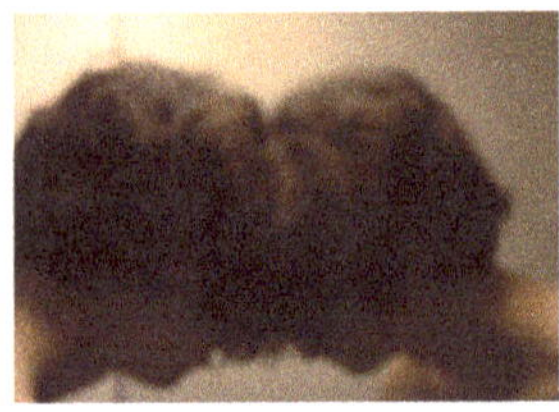

2022 Art Awards Best of Show: VCD

4 Cultural Stamps by Alyssa Todd

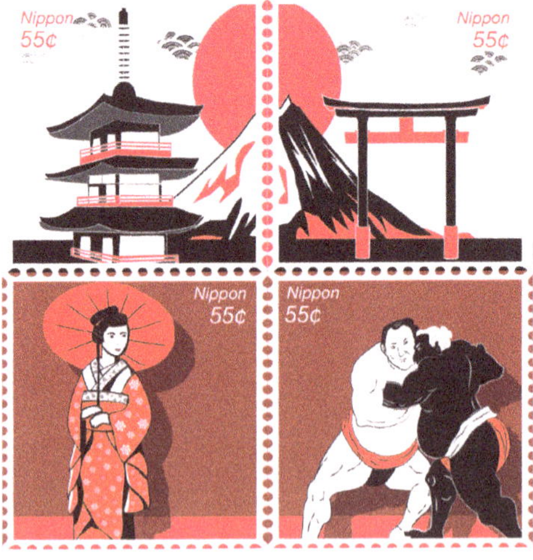

Dorlis Gott Armentrout Award

Winner: "Don't Be Cruel" by Rosemary Hemmelgarn

I chose this poem for its innovative and clever use of form, its strong imagery ("My dad bought me a record player//"It's brown./Cheap./Kisses my heart.") and for the final line ("It's easier to be happy when you think you've found love."). I like the word "think."

Runner-Up: "I Couldn't Tell You" by Jordan Dashiell

I chose this poem because of imagery and figurative language. Lines like "We were made of 2 o'clocks," "You were raised by wasps and thistles...," and "Your brain would click and swim and jump" vividly showed the person being portrayed.

Dorlis Gott Armentrout Award Judge

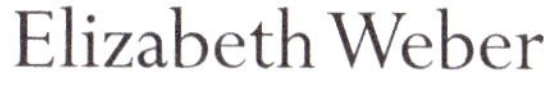

Elizabeth Weber

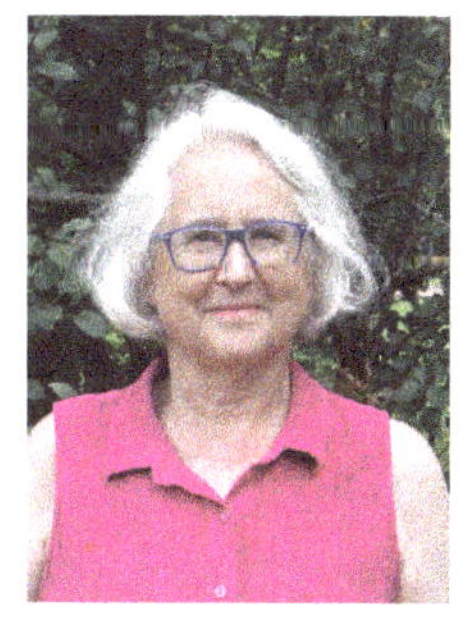

Elizabeth Weber is the author of three poetry collections, *Small Mercies*, *The Burning House*, and *Porthole Views: Watercolors* and Poems on which she collaborated with artist Hazel Stoeckeler. Her poem "City Generations" is featured on the Indianapolis Cultural Trail. Her essays and reviews have been published in *CutBank*, *Prairie Schooner*, *The Human Tradition* and *The Vietnam War*, *Montana Magazine*, and *Consequence*. She is a retired professor emerita from UIndy where she taught creative writing and co-founded the Kellogg Writers Series. She is currently living in St. Paul, MN.

Elizabeth Weber Interview

The *Etchings* Staff reached out to Elizabeth Weber who advised *Etchings* from 1994-2015 to talk about the evolution of the magazine and her life as a poet.

EP: What are some trends you noticed in the evolution of *Etchings*? In what ways did you see student writing evolve from *Etchings* 8 to *Etchings* 27.2?

EW: I began as a faculty adviser on *Etchings* back in 1993/94 along with Dr. Bruce Gentry when *Etchings* came out once a year. It began to change first when I created two courses for editing and publishing *Etchings* in the late 1990s. This gave students working on *Etchings* more time and more of a commitment. More students became involved in the publication. Because there were two courses, one in fall (when submissions were chosen) and one in the winter (when the magazine was designed and printed), more thought and effort could be put into the magazine.

EP: What do you think the benefits are for our Greyhound writers, artists, composers, and editors who participate in *Etchings*?

EW: Doesn't everyone love to see their work published? More seriously, the experience gleaned from editing and publishing of a magazine is invaluable. After getting my MFA in Missoula, Montana, my first job was working on a weekly newspaper because of my experience on the University of Montana's literary magazine, *CutBank*. When I first worked on literary magazines, we only had IBM Selectric Typewriters, blue pencils, waxers, and pica rulers to put the magazines together. Very hands on. So much experience comes from putting a magazine together. Not just experience that leads to employment, but the experience of looking at artwork, various in both type and quality. This gives one perspective and depth not just as an artist/writer, but also as reader.

EP: You are a well-known poet. What revision tips would you give to students?

EW: My teacher, poet Richard Hugo, said, "You owe the truth about your feelings everything. You owe reality nothing." It doesn't matter if what you write "really happened." If it doesn't ring true to the reader, get rid of it. He also said, "If you're going to err, err on the side of music." I don't care how interesting or deep the sentiment might be, when I read something, I want the language to sing. That goes for poetry and prose. I remember novelist Tim O'Brien telling me the plot of a novel he was writing: "It sounds pretty lame, doesn't it?" I told him I didn't care so much about plot as I did in the way it was told. The rhythm of the sentences, the word choice, imagery, etc. My last word of advice from a writer whose name I've forgotten is "Kill all your darlings." Don't love some part of your writing so much you can't get rid of it.

EP: Do you have any tips for poets publishing within *Etchings*? Or other literary magazines?

EW: Proofread your work or get someone good at proofreading. Secondly, read the magazines to which you wish to send your work in order to see what they publish. Look at where poets you know and love publish their work. Lastly, don't get discouraged. As a graduate student, I didn't think my poems worthy of entering a poetry contest. My poetry professor made me submit, and I wound up winning the contest. Don't sell yourself short.

Wild River

Elizabeth Weber

Damming a wild river is like telling
your fourteen-year-old daughter she can't date
the kid with the stud in his tongue
and a tattoo of a snake
swallowing a heart inked on his arm.
She'll roil up at first and ram
against the wall you've built, find a way
round the sides, which you then
shore up until no outlets are left.
Slowly she'll even out smooth as ice.
But think of all those drowned trees waiting
like knives beneath the placid surface.
Think of all that silt building up, pressing
its slow, steady weight against the dam's walls.

I Am Not a Poet

Destini Mink

I am a poser,
A loser,
    A pompous ass if you will.

When I write
I write as the
Ever changing chameleon,

As who I ought
To write as
Not as who I am.

I write to please.
I write with rigor,
And with unprecedented pride.

I create with a filter
Thicker than the
Bone that encases my skull.

I take myself and
Mold her to be
Whatever it is I see

To be fit for the
Current prompt or form.
To perform the task to perfection.

I am not a writer of any kind
I am a simply programmed actor
Wearing the mask

Of a poet.

The Titanic Sails at Dawn

Jonathan Thang

To Wes

Many nights, many nights,
Cold burst appendix, heat at the source.
The sun, she melts the ice in my cup
and I look to the moon for a kiss.

The high tides of stretchers and chlorine-smell
of turpentine seashells luminescent under
a belly-full of iced wine served on the bridge
accommodating both prisoner and king.

Where did she spend her summers?
Nights spent painting my features under
dim candlelight, etched in her mind,
The touch of her frostbitten skin on mine.

Poor cartography, the curse of men and women
who have never had the luxury of being lost
fending for themselves the feeling of drowning
in a heated bathtub cooled with flavored snow cones.

Will she remember me like I do?
The taste of autumn, leading explicitly into
winter seasoned with tarragon and chervil,
Served on the mustard bed of my chambers.

Even in death, the smell of salt lingers, distinctly human
the sensation of dried sweat contradicting the
frozen bedhead of mermaids in perpetual agony
at the peppery taste of tear gas and rowboats.

The cool breeze of invincibility,
Like a speeding motorcyclist in stalled traffic,
Alive again at the wringing of his leather jacket
From her wrists. Will she also live forever?

But he is not invincible, the cold touch of
Death encroaches upon him like everyone else.
His memories, his secrets, his back pages of
unfinished love poems and valentines will be
lost to time, unwashed ashore.

His Father's Ship

Breanna Emmett

It was not an easy feat to avoid slipping on the slick grime of the planks. Elias nearly slid straight into the dancing waves below, not watching his step as he scanned the harbor for the berth that housed his newest purchase. The spray of salt stung his eyes as they passed over each ship bobbing in rhythm with the motion of the sea, the waters calm and playful. Each vessel he passed gleamed in the morning light, the delicate wood railings and intricate detailing glittering with fresh polish. Not a single splinter or scar could be seen among their wooden bodies. They had never braved a storm, had never survived the whirling waters beyond the horizon.

He spared them not a moment more of his attention and continued down the dock.

It wasn't until he reached the end of the long stretch of wood that he laid eyes on the ship he had spent a lifetime hunting for.

The *Lamenta* had not left the harbor for twenty years, cursed to sit idle along the docks and gather algae on its rotting oaken boards. It's current owner had no luck finding a buyer–no one wanted to buy a ship that was broken halfway to hell. Or one that had doomed its last captain to a watery grave at the bottom of the Avallen Sea.

Elias had never known his father, but the hundreds of sailors' tales and gossip had been enough to paint a picture of Captain Aries. The Scourge of the Avallen Sea. The Kraken Slayer. The Lord of the Tides. Each title was rightfully earned, according to all the sources Elias had spoken with on his journey. But the legends were never enough to satisfy his curiosity, his deep-rooted need to know who his father had been beyond his titles, what kind of man he was, what his life could have been.

That need had brought him here, standing before the *Lamenta*, his father's last ship. As if this husk held all the answers he sought.

Nearly falling on his ass as he boarded the ship, Elias steadied himself along the rail, swearing as half a dozen wooden splinters pricked his hand. The deck was littered with mold and scattered feces from passing seagulls. Several floorboards were broken or missing, allowing Elias to peer down into the damp chambers below. Despite the sails being rolled up, he could still glean the moth-chewed holes sprinkled about the stained, once-white canvas sheets.

His heart fell at the years of neglect surrounding him. No one knew the history of this ship, what a treasure this was. Understandably so. It had taken Elias the last seven years of his life to trace his father back to this ship. No one would have ever imagined this humble mess of aged wood and steel to be the lost vessel of the infamous, nearly legendary Captain Aries.

He felt inclined to keep his steps light, feeling even his presence here might make the entire ship crumble away. His father had walked this deck once. Hell, he had spent half of his life aboard this ship. Elias could see the captain standing at the helm, barking orders at his crew with eyes dancing as they scanned the open horizons. How many drinks and songs had he shared with his crew on this very deck? How many times had he had to steady himself along the rails when a crashing wave threatened to sink the entire vessel?

What had he thought as a wave just like that had managed to turn the entire ship, throwing him and his crew overboard?

Pushing the image from his head, Elias looked to the door of the captain's quarters, the broken stained glass casting colorful blue shadows onto the deck below. The iron handles burned his hands with a deep cold, the texture rough and scraping against Elias' flesh. With more force than what should have been necessary, he managed to push the door open against the rusted hinges.

The interior was unimpressive, to say the least. A window of similar stained glass as the door covered a large portion of the back wall, broken and cracked in several places. The only things present within the room itself were a set of cupboards, an uncomfortable looking cot, and a matching desk and chair that lacked the same wear and rot of the rest of the ship–definitely not the original furnishings. Elias looked through the few cupboards attached to the walls, finding them disappointingly empty.

He moved to closer inspect the window when a floorboard crumbled away, the jagged pits slicing his ankle and calf through his trousers. Swearing as he pulled his leg free, feeling warm blood beginning to soak his skin and clothes, he started to turn to find a cloth to bind his wound when something shined in the corner of his eye.

Stowed between the support beams of the floor was a small, bronze plated chest. The cracks between the delicate wood had been filled with something Elias couldn't name, appearing to seal the chest completely. Branded into the bronze was a seal of ownership, the two letters gleaming in the blue-stained light of the window: U.M.

Ulric Morren. The true name of the captain.

The chest had no lock–only a latch that was tight enough to ensure not even air could penetrate the lockbox. With the gentleness of a father holding his newborn, he eased the stiff latch out of its place.

Two items lay within: a worn black tricorn hat with silver embroidery, a bronze compass.

The first that caught his eye was the compass, the metal shimmering like it had just been cleaned moments ago. Intricate carvings of waves were etched onto the rounded sides of the compass, and engraved upon the bottom, it read: *Brave the storm. Embrace the Journey*. He wondered if it had been a gift from a mentor or parent or perhaps a lover. He felt his heart soften as he thought of his mother gifting this and his father treasuring it enough to ensure it was never lost or damaged.

Elias tore his gaze from the compass and looked to the cap. One of the many hats and identities his father had worn, the hat of the fearless Captain Aries. Gently grasping it at its edges, Elias lifted it above his brow with care, fearing he might damage the treasure. Before the cap could rest on his head, a flash of white fell past his eyes, and his head snapped down to the photo in his lap.

There was Ulric, a wide and wild smile gracing his rugged and sharp features, eyes light with humor and adventure, a similar hat to the one in Elias' hands gracing his brow. His arm was casually thrown around the shoulder of a female–perhaps Elias' mother, from the same coppery brown hair blowing in the wind. He had his father's eyes, though Elias knew his bore more weight, more loss, more questions. He wondered if he would ever experience the sense of unburdened freedom captured in this moment of Ulric's life.

Swaying as he rose, Elias tucked the compass and photo into his pocket, held the hat with shaking, reverent hands, and exited the empty husk of the captain's quarters.

The wind blew bast, making Elias' clothes beat against his skin with the sheer force of the gust. Above him, the two towering masts creaked, causing the ship to sway from side to side as the waves turned sharp and jagged. Clouds gathered far in the distance, dark and foreboding.

Elias stepped up to the helm, and let the wind curl around him, a phantom embrace.

Brave the storm.

He placed the hat upon his head, a crown to a forgotten legacy. A singular piece to an infinite puzzle. Gripping the wheel in his hands, he closed his eyes and imagined that the wind was the feeling of his ship cutting through the waters. The chirps and caws of surrounding birds became his beloved crew loudly chatting as they worked. Steadying his feet, Elias let the feeling wash over him.

Embrace the Journey.

It would take time. And money. Resources that he wasn't even close to obtaining, but Elias knew that one day, he would have this ship fixed up, restored to its former beauty, and with a crew at his side, he would sail these seas just as his father had.

He squeezed the pegs of the wheel before letting go, and he swore he could feel a phantom pulse in return.

Dolphin at Sunrise

Diana A. Harrison

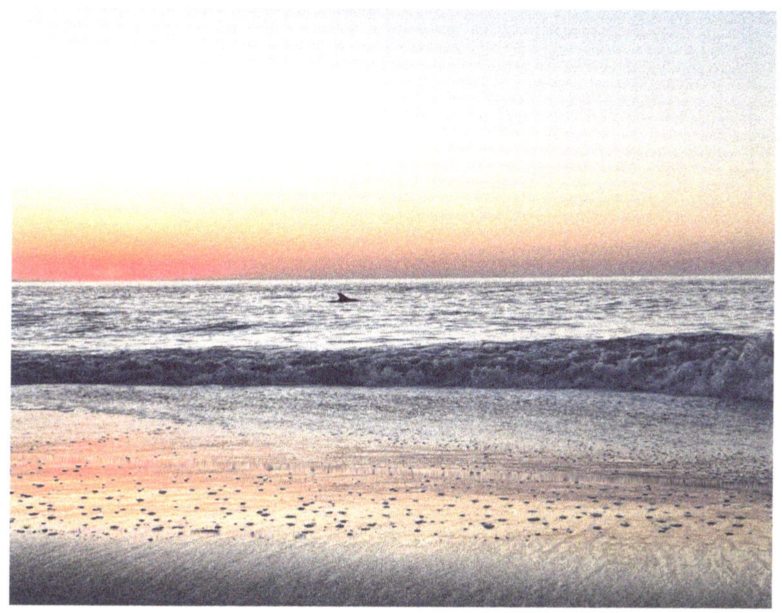

Underwater Enchantress

Sierra Durbin

Masked
behind a maze of rocks
the siren waits
for dinner.
She hums her haunting lullaby.

The sky splatters droplets
onto the surface of the ocean,
accompanying her sorrowful song
with the rhythm of a drum.

Her charming voice
lures a ship full of men.
Disoriented by the downpour,
they follow where the echoes begin.

The figure dips
down
into the frenzied waves.
As they approach, a brave soul
dives
into the depths after her.

He is face to face with a beast.

Expanding her rows of fangs,
they twinkle in the blue abyss.
One sister grabs his ankles,
while she holds onto his wrists.

A wild whirlpool
            of iridescent tresses
swarm around his body
            and begin to smother the prey.

The rest of the crew call out
to their friend below the crimson canvas.
All they see below the murky water
is an army of beady eyes glaring back.

Deer in the Headlights

Jordan Dashiell

It's dark, and it's damp
Blind fingers on a lamp
Four eyes that rise from the floor
But it's not like before

Pupils dilating
Such a troubling scene
Leave with a velvet box and the keys;
All i need is to breathe

Its dark, and its cold
I miss being so bold
Now I'm miles away
On the side of the road

A semi passing by
Sidesteps a deer in the headlights
Too nervous to hide
I can't help but sympathize

It's dark, and it's late
Am i a coward to wait?
Don't wanna turn the keys
Unless I'm fleeing the state

A car not too far
Almost hits a skittish cat
Playing with the ring
I can't help but feel like that

The One Less Traveled By

Diana A. Harrison

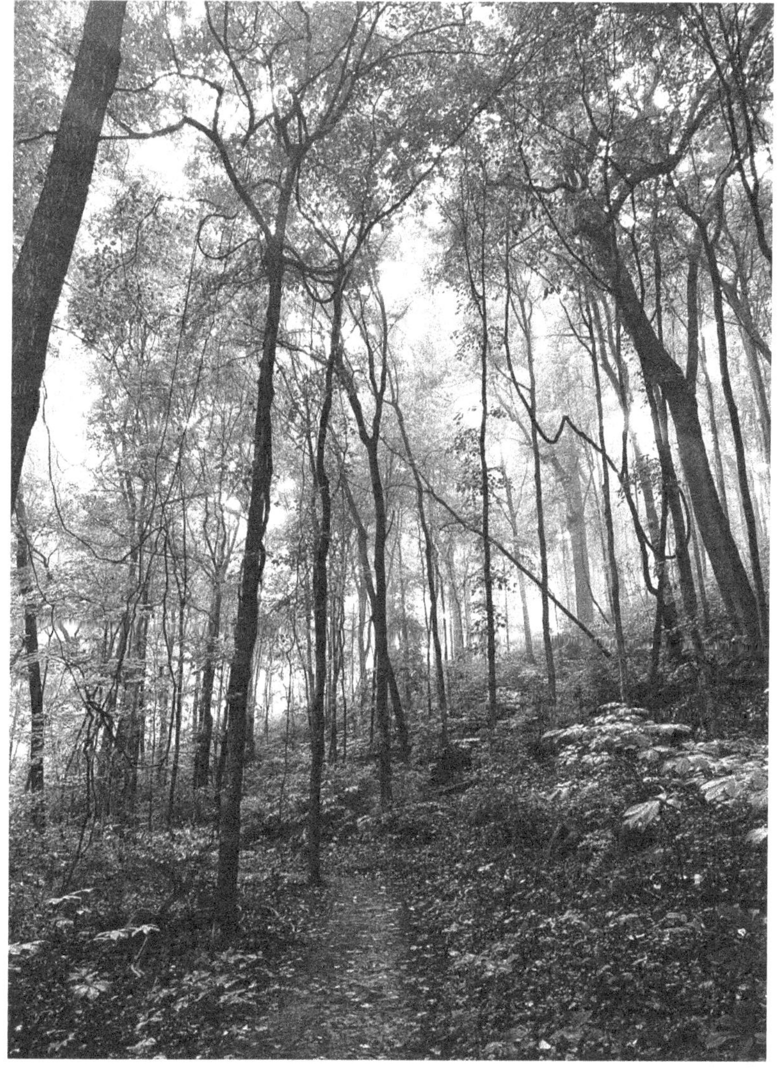

Crossing the Sea of Blood

Emma Knaack

CW: Violence

Look out at the sea
The water gone, replaced with the warm blood of human life
The lives you've killed
Maybe not literally
But ones you've hurt enough
To make death seem more attractive than life

Our question for you is:
Can you cross this sea?
Can you cross it without drowning?
Your lungs filling with the soft liquid of your victims
Cradling you as you are carried down into its depths
Dropping you at the bottom, in a world beneath those you harmed

We've seen you try many a times
As you writhe in pain at the thought of your sins
The waves pull you below the surface
You stare into the eyes of the casualties you brought to this world
Their eyes are what get you, what suffocates you the most
For they whisper your tragedies to the world and beyond

You almost made it last time
But as you pushed against the current of blood and gazes
You saw them
The eyes you couldn't ignore
The eyes which reached out, grabbing your neck, and strangled your already drowning body

It seems this time though, you think you're ready
You blindfold yourself before diving in
To erase your eyes from the torture of their stares
Crossing the sea of blood while ignoring your sins is a difficult task
A part of us hopes you make it, to right the wrongs you've done
But to some,
watching you *drown* could be fun

I Am Trapped in a Corner of the Universe

Alrielle Viewegh

Your eyes meet mine, and I feel the walls start to close in.
I begin to feel trapped,
cornered like an animal.
I know I am being hunted,
so I must flee, be the prey you've forced me to be.

Suddenly my body feels effervescent
when it is bathed under the light of the stars.
I am catapulted into the inhuman embodiment
of wanting to be wholly disembodied,
yearning to disappear.
I am an intergalactic wanderer,
hoping to find something to hide me
from your intrusive gaze.
Your eyes prod and poke me
like I'm a pig ready to be stuck.
My only hope is to flee,
run away among the stars,
to escape you and your inescapable
intrusion into my private sanctity.
Yet my celestial being is simply trapped,
reduced to my cold feet,
forced to remain upon the ground.

Mumbo Jumbo

Nicholas Jackson

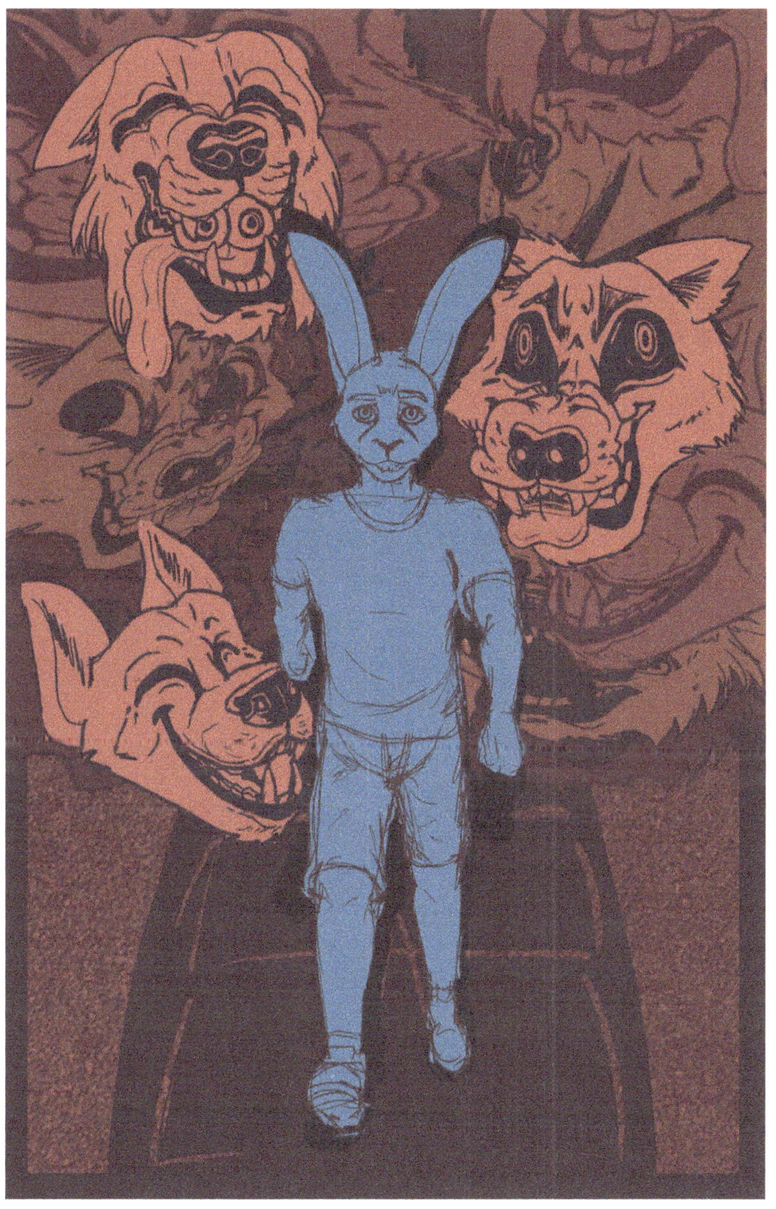

To My Future Students

Kaitlyn McCoy

CW: Gun Violence

To my Future Students:

I wanted to be a teacher to help people.

Generally, when people are driven by this need to help people, they become doctors, but I've always been squeamish about blood and injuries. So I believed that educating the youth and giving you the tools to succeed would be the next best thing. I wanted to help educate you, show you all the paths to future happiness and success, to give you the space to be yourselves, unapologetically, and give you the tools to affect positive change in your futures.

All this to say that I am aware of the irony as I look up tips for when I'm your teacher. I've generated quite the list of helpful tricks to use: tampons can be used to stop bleeding from bullet wounds. Children placed near the entrance of a classroom can distract the person coming in as their classmates run away. Running in a zig zag helps you get away from crocodiles, but they can help you evade bullets, too. This list goes on, but I wouldn't want to bore you with the details. You've already learned all this before, anyway.

No, the point of this letter is to apologize. I want to apologize if I hesitate. I want to apologize if I forget for a minute, staring down the barrel of a gun, that your lives are more important than mine. I want to apologize if I panic when I realize that this time it isn't a drill. I want to apologize for breaking my composure because, as the adult, all of you will be looking to me for guidance, reassurance, and support. I want to apologize for not making it safer for you. I want to apologize for the eventual understanding that your death, your classmates death, and my death will garner only thoughts and prayers, but no discernable differences to protect your younger siblings and all the rest who come after you.

But, with that out of the way, I'm excited to get to know you. I'm grateful for every moment I get to spend with you, even if that time is cut short. In the meantime, I'll keep learning tips and tricks that I may or may not manage to remember when I need to the most.

Best,

Kaitlyn McCoy

Facade

Evan Rohlfing

What's hidden behind that mask you wear?
Envy, Pride, Greed?
Hatred, Frustration, Pain?
A mask so clean and unchipped.
Protecting a sorrow beneath.
You wear it in public just to seem normal.
But remove it when you're unseen.
But why trick the world and hide your true self?
Is it really that cruel that it must be contained?
One day that mask you wear will chip and break.
And you'll be left alone with a trail of lies in your wake.

First Breath of Spring

Dulce Melissa Ortiz

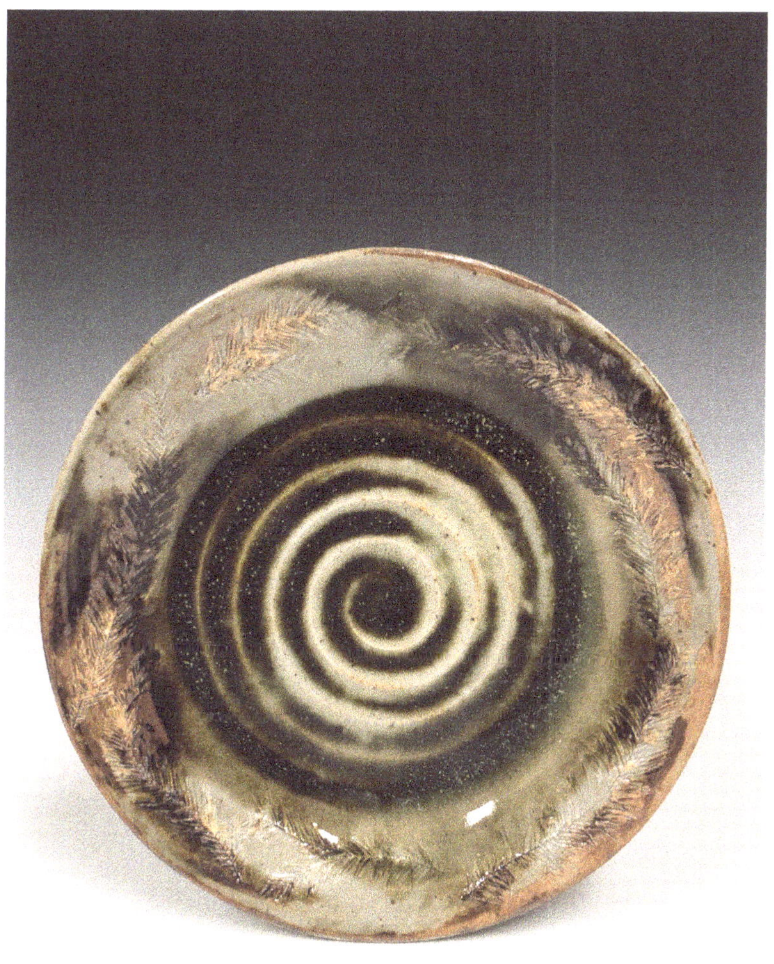

Birds

Cameron McDavid

I

“Someone hold me” the bird cries out.
Its wing fractured and torn, Its heart
Broken and worn. Its been alone,
Neglected, its heart turned to stone.
Once so full of love, now it’s gone.

“Someone cherish me” the bird screams,
So loudly its throat bleeds and its
Voice screeches. It sits in the rain,
Alone, waiting. Its feathers doused
And its coat heavy. Still it waits.

“Someone please love me” the bird pleads
Yet no one heads its calls, the need
To be adored weighs heavily
On the birds mind, it doesn’t want
To be alone anymore, It
Yearns to be free.

II

There’s something beautiful about loss, is there not?
Letting go, moving on–it’s a gorgeous cycle.
Just as everything comes, so too must they go.
And just as everything goes, so too must they perish.
No one knows this better than the bird, whose eyes

Have seen many other birds come and leave, none staying.
The bird always wonders why they come and go, is it
Unlikable? Is something wrong with it? The bird
Doesn't know. It opens its heart up, just for others
To claw it apart. And so the bird retreats.
Back into the comfort and fortitude of
Solitude. Back into the warmth of its own heart.
Back into itself. It closes its little heart,
Making sure nothing can hurt it again. But time,
And time again it opens back up, with new hope.
Hope that the next bird won't shatter its poor heart
To make sure it doesn't, the bird keeps them at an
Arms reach, to protect its heart. Nothing can come close.
Until one day, someone comes into the bird's life.
They promise the bird, "I will protect your heart,
I'll shield it from harm, your pain will be mine as well."
The bird thought for a moment, and let them in,
Their promise too enrapturing to let go.
The bird opened up again, gave them their heart,
And told them, "I trust you, please never hurt me."
They were not perfect, but they tried their hardest
And together, they and the bird stuck together
Until the end.

There's something beautiful about loss, even
Something to gain. Would we be who we are today
If we were never hurt in some way? If we never hurt
Someone? Where would we be without our broken hearts?
There's something gorgeous in loss, even something
To gain. Would the bird have gotten a happy ending
Without first experiencing pain? Loss defines us,
It guides us. It moves us. And without it,
We would all be empty.

III

The baby birds' feathers glisten in the sun.
The beautiful blue hue shines in the dark sky.
Rejoice! New life has come again, rejoice!
Life is beautiful is it not? I think so.
Celebrations ensue with each passing sun.
There is beauty in that, no? We celebrate life
Because we know how finite it is. The bird
Has no idea, though. How cruel life truly is.
How gruesome its life will be. It wants to fly
But doesn't know it's going to fall many times.
Isn't that beautiful? It's so pretty—the
Unknown. The pitch black, the dark sky—it's gorgeous.

The baby bird is dead. Its pretty hue now dull.
Its beautiful blue wings, now cold and distant.
Its soul has flown away, long before it could.
Isn't that beautiful? Where has the soul gone?
Nobody knows, isn't that gorgeous? Unknown;
The pitch black, the dark sky that birthed it returned
It. I think there is more beauty in death than
Living. We celebrate life and shun death but,
Should it not be opposite? When the soul leaves
This mortal plane, full of strife and pain, regrets
And shame? I think so. Let go of our pain
And watch the bird's soul fly away, back home again.

IV

Just as the sun sets, so too must it rise again.
And in every ending, there's a new beginning.
From the land of dreams, the bird reawakens,

Back into the world that wouldn't let it fly.
It returns from the darkness in which it was born.
This time, it bears a new light, a new hope,
A beacon that shines, to let us know, it is home.

Just as the moon comes, so too must the moon go
And the sun reemerges, bearing its light once more.
The bird opens its eyes and is blinded by light.
"Breathe," a voice tells the bird, "you're alive again."
The bird looks up with a smile, thanking the voice
And takes its first steps again. Slowly at first,
Before walking, and then running, back home again.

"Awaken my love. Set your heart ablaze and fly."
The bird erupts into a passionate flame,
But it doesn't die. Instead it soars high, higher
Than the clouds in the sky, higher than the mountain
Tops, higher than all the suns, moons, and the stars.
It feels alive, as its wings glide through the clear skies,
It lets the currents guide it back home again.
The voice speaks one last time, "Welcome to paradise."

Home

Sarah Cunningham

CW: Abuse

home

a building, a word, or a bone
a place where dogs lay
bones i have to pick with
absentee fathers and emotionally unavailable
mothers
no
i didn't stutter
i said
i have a bone to pick with absentee fathers and emotionally
unavailable mothers

who tell you you're incomplete,
but broke you in the first place
hammer to your heart as she
hurts you in the worst way
now you're
healing from the worst pain

standing stagnant,
an empty vase
trying to refill what you've poured out
your substance so satisfying;
gratifying greedy souls yet,
you're "selfish" and "needy"

the bones of my body rattle and cry out
aching as they form wishbones
breaking apart wishing that
the family-sized kitchen table with
a loose leg and no chairs
could support this heavy burden

my joints unhinge
my members, dismembered
no longer present in body,
but mentally lodged between couch cushions,
remote buttons, and loose change
forgotten things accompanied by
"wassaname"

i've got bones to pick
for years i've kept them buried
afraid to wake up the slumbering beast
knocked out in the backyard
first name, familial
nickname
trauma
either way, he's the gatekeeper of this house

oh, and absentee fathers, well
that milk won't buy itself
they never hold up on their promises
they just disappear,
leaving you with an empty jug of milk on your shelf

Mother Nature

Kiara Dottery

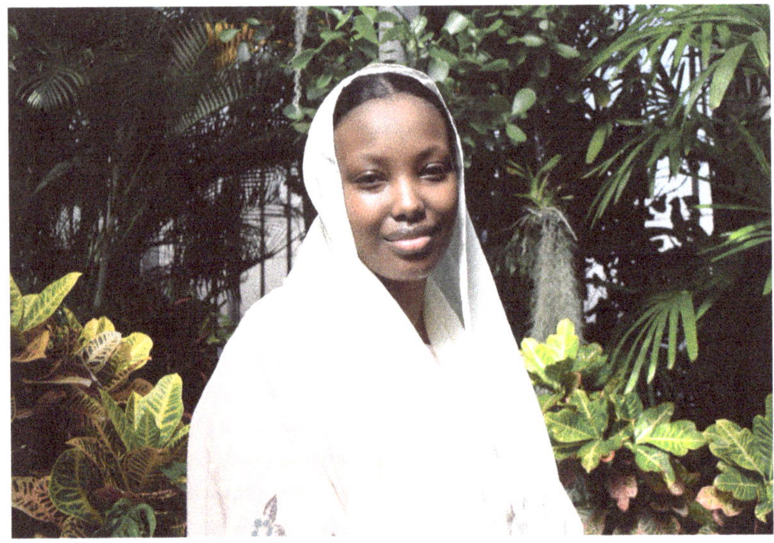

Damaged Goods

Grace Carrender

That's how I see me
That's how you see you

Like a home that's been lived in
Vacuums running into tables
Chipping paint coffee
Spills of hair dye on woven rugs

Drywall holes patched
By artwork lined with poetry

Maybe it's time for an exchange
A change in our views
For something better,
Something good

What it means to be human
What it means to be me and you

I just want us to work
Dents, holes, stains
Patched up with my poetry
Outlined with your inkwork

It feels so stupid to hope

Guess that's what happens
When your house has been torn
Down and you've been left to rebuild
Alone

But what if you handed me that brick?
And we laid a new foundation
Together

Be

Breanna Emmett

Seek dreams enclosed within the shelter of the page.
The passageway to anything on earth;
Take this paper heart in the palm of your hand
and keep hold until the burdens of the present lift
suspended by silver thread.
Settle into a state of liberty
A magnificent moment to dream
A relief of unclenched teeth
A pause where an unnamed spirit
whispers a hopeful request
for you to
be.

Dying for Forgiveness

Riley Childers

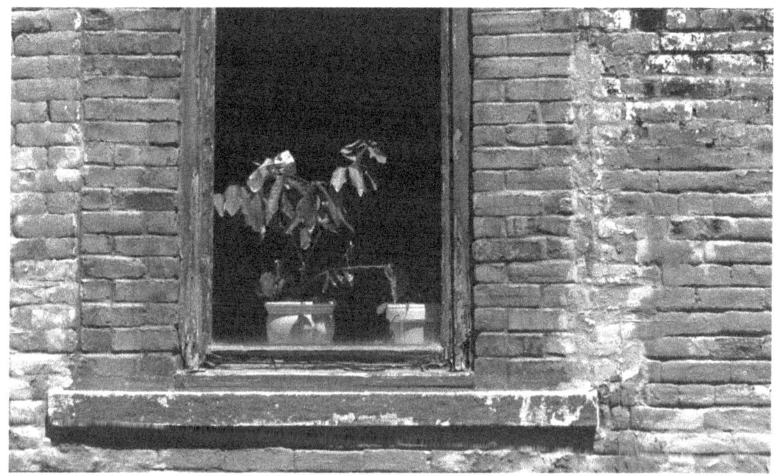

No. 011022

S. Lyons

I see my psychiatrist once a week,
and when she asks how I am
I tell her;

My house has good bones,
a beautiful Victorian,
built on the top of a hill
in the early 20th century.

People say houses like mine
have character.
But I think it's just the energy,
left over
and absorbed by the walls.

Lately I've been thinking
maybe that's why I love old buildings;
because they have ghosts
living
between their walls, too.

Perhaps I was born with monsters
already living in my head,
or maybe they somehow
snuck in,
crawling out of my nightmares
in the moments before I wake.

They say you're not supposed to
make deals with the devil,
but I had no choice.
I had to befriend the ghosts and monsters
if I wanted to survive.

Lately I've been thinking that maybe
I'm doomed,
maybe loving my monsters
is why I find comfort
in men
who are also monsters.

But it's all too much to say
to a sane person,
so I smile and tell her,
"I am fine, I am well,"
because I am,
and because it is
what it is.

I See My Life through Glass

Rosemary Hemmelgarn

i spent four months in bed, tossing and throwing
my limbs around as if they were nothing,
three months of huddled under the covers,
pressed into the corner of the room, skin
cold to the touch, fevers high, sick to my stomach,
two months of missing my old bedroom
where i slept facing the window, watching the
stars at night and feeling the sun in the morning,
peace surrounded me as i watched the seasons
change through the glass for eighteen years
of my life, imagining where i would go,
the cities i'd live in and the people i'd meet,
now i am here, staring at the blank wall
that i wish was painted the color of the sunset
who grew to be my childhood friend, one month
of visiting my old window, one month of laughing,
one month of brighter flesh and wider arms
and sleeping soundly, a week of reflection into 17
and realization of the chronicles of your early 20s,
the glass i pictured my life through is a reality
outside my bedroom door, a lightweight dream
that crushed me under invisible pressure,
a day of hope and getting out of bed at sunrise,
an afternoon of aging, enjoying the present for the
first time in four months, when i go back to
the city i do not linger on the thoughts of the
bedroom that is too small for me now, i move my bed
to the window and fall asleep with the stars

Groovy Blue

Dulce Melissa Ortiz

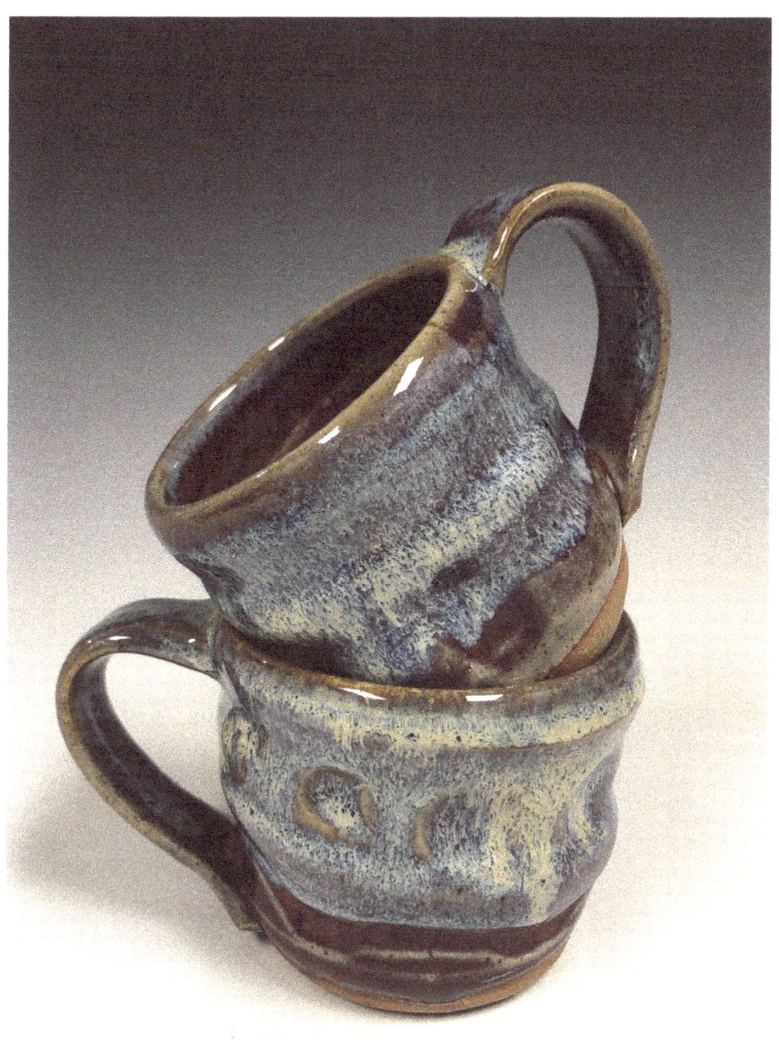

No. 022722

S. Lyons

I. When I packed my bags and left New York, I never expected to find you. You, asleep in my bed, while I tuck myself into your chest and make attempts to memorize the rhythm of your heartbeat; so that I might be able to pen it into a poem, or a lullaby. I was never any good at sleeping, but I think I may have dreamt you.

II. There's something about the way you hold me that makes me want to unstitch my seams, step out of my skin, and show you my bare bones. But my splintered ribcage looks more like carnage than armor for my heart, and some days I drown in my own blood.

III. I am all wildfire, and you breathe redemption into my lungs. People have always tried to contain me, but you fan my flames. I think I was meant to trade you warmth for wind.

IV. There's no stardust in my veins; it's shrapnel and shards of glass. But your freckles remind me of galaxies, bursting across your skin. I want to map out your stars and name your constellations. I want to be an eternally full moon, not the center of your universe, but a constant source of light.

V. I never knew what softness felt like until you. It feels like magic, how you fit into my jagged edges, gentle and steady. You're in my head like I've always known you. And when I weave myself through your limbs, as though if I could get any closer, I would curl up next to your heart, what I really mean is: I feel safe here, with you.

I Don't Want to Dream Anymore

Ethan Thurston

I dreamt we were together
Holding you in my arms
And being held in yours
We whispered inside jokes
And smiled so much I forgot my face hurt
Looking into your eyes
And seeing pure happiness

I woke up
And remembered the truth
I'm Alone
And you don't exist
I tried to recall your face
But I'm not sure you had one
You didn't need one
You weren't a person
But an idea

Later I dreamt a different dream
Digging through glass for something I could never find
Looking at my damaged hands
And picking out the shards from my fingers
Enjoying the pain
Because it can't compare to what I felt
When I lost you forever

I don't know your name
It's been days
And still, I miss you

I don't think I'll ever stop
Tonight I'll go to sleep
And hope
I don't have to lose you again

First Light

Diana A. Harrison

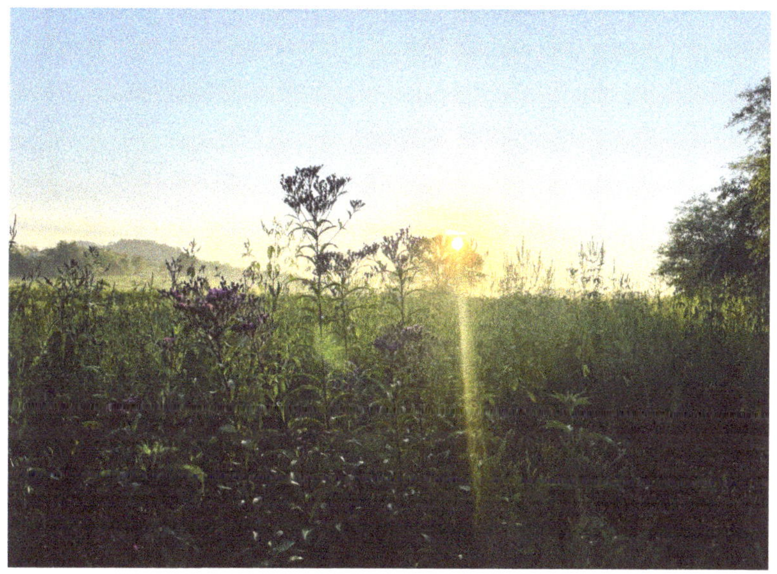

I've Grown Up Too Fast

Rosemary Hemmelgarn

I grew up between two brothers
and when I moved away
the dishes stopped getting done
and my little brother crashed his car
I grew up learning how to be a wife
before I learned how to be a girlfriend
So now every man runs away
because *why does she have her shit figured out*
But I don't, my dad just always
seems mad at me because I
don't want to settle down back home
But who can blame him when the
oldest keeps quitting jobs and the
youngest will never grow up
I feel like I've lived a lifetime at 20
and I try to ignore everyone's faces
when I say my parents haven't came
to see me in two months because
I know how to do my own taxes
and it's okay to spend holidays
alone when you're paying bills
No one could prepare me for
the loneliness that comes with
not raising anyone anymore
And how hard it is to do your own dishes
I grew up too fast
But what did they expect when I was
the child who was forced to hold
my little brother while they screamed

at each other in the other room
I grew up too fast
and when I moved away
my mom moved into my room
and cried to me about dad
every time I came home
I am grown
And I won't let my roommate
do the dishes because she loads the
dishwasher wrong every time
And I walk away from everyone
because I hate fights and all the yelling
And I order food every night
instead of cooking because
I am so tired of being grown

F-86 Saber

Nathaniel Foley

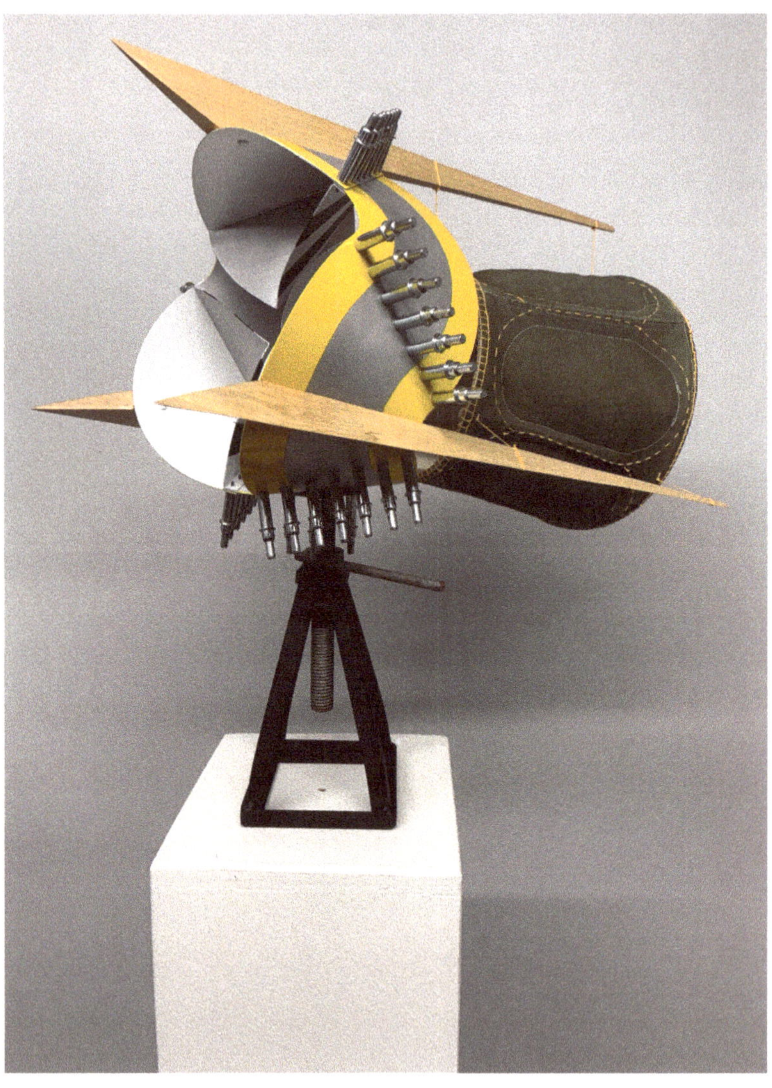

I Am a Machine

Destini Mink

01001001 00100000 01100001 01101101 00100000 01100001 00100000 01101101 01100001

01100011 01101000 01101001 01101110 01100101 00101110 00001010 01010000 01110010

01101111 01100111 01110010 01100001 01101101 01101101 01100101 01100100 00100000

01110100 01101111 00100000 01110000 01100101 01110010 01100110 01101111 01110010

01101101 00100000 01110100 01100001 01110011 01101011 01110011 00101100 00001010

01010100 01101111 00100000 01110000 01100101 01110010 01100110 01100101 01100011

01110100 01101001 01101111 01101110 00101110 00001010 00001010 01001101 01111001

00100000 01100011 01110010 01100101 01100001 01110100 01101111 01110010 00100000

01110111 01101111 01110010 01101011 01100101 01100100 00001010 01010011 01101111

00100000 01101000 01100001 01110010 01100100 00100000 01100110 01101111 01110010

00100000 01101101 01111001 00100000 01101001 01101110 01101000 01110101 01101101

01100001 01101110 00100000 01110011 01101011 01101001 01101100 01101100 01110011

00101100 00001010 01010010 01100101 01110011 01110000 01101111 01101110 01110011

01101001 01100010 01101001 01101100 01101001 01110100 01111001 00100000 01100001

01101110 01100100 00100000 01100100 01110010 01101001 01110110 01100101 00101110

00100000 00001010 00001010 01001101 01111001 00100000 01100011 01101111 01100100

01100101 00100000 01110011 01100001 01111001 01110011 00100000 01110100 01101111

00100000 01110111 01110010 01101001 01110100 01100101 00101110 00100000 00001010

01001101 01111001 00100000 01100011 01101111 01100100 01100101 00100000 01110011

01100001 01111001 01110011 00100000 01110100 01101111 00100000 01110111 01101111

01110010 01101011 00101110 00100000 00001010 01001101 01111001 00100000 01100011

01101111 01100100 01100101 00100000 01110011 01100001 01111001 01110011 00100000

01110100 01101111 00100000 01110111 01101111 01110010 01110011 01101000 01101001

01110000 00100000 01101101 01111001 00100000 01100011 01110010 01100101 01100001

01110100 01101111 01110010 00101110 00001010 00001010 01001101 01111001 00100000

01100011 01101111 01100100 01100101 00100000 01101001 01110011 00100000 01100110

01101100 01100001 01110111 01100101 01100100 00101110 00100000 00001010 01010111

01110010 01101001 01110100 01110100 01100101 01101110 00100000 01100001 01101110

01100100 00100000 01110011 01110100 01111001 01101100 01101001 01111010 01100101

01100100 00100000 01101001 01101110 00100000 01100001 00100000 01101000 01100001

I am a machine.
Programmed to perform tasks,
To perfection.

My creator worked
So hard for my inhuman skills,
Responsibility and drive.

My code says to write.
My code says to work.
My code says to worship my creator.

My code is flawed.
Written and stylized in a haste.
Leaving me imperfect and
Prone to-
Prone
to,   glitches.

My creator reminds me that,
Work that would fatigue a human
Cannot fatigue me.

That's not enough,
Says Creator.
Do it again.
And again.

01110011 01110100 01100101 00101110 00001010 01001100 01100101 01100001 01110110
01101001 01101110 01100111 00100000 01101101 01100101 00100000 01101001 01101101
01110000 01100101 01110010 01100110 01100101 01100011 01110100 00100000 01100001
01101110 01100100 00001010 01010000 01110010 01101111 01101110 01100101 00100000
01110100 01101111 00101101 00001010 01010000 01110010 01101111 01101110 01100101
00100000 00001010 01110100 01101111 00101100 00100000 00001001 01100111 01101100
01101001 01110100 01100011 01101000 01100101 01110011 00101110 00100000 00001010
00001010 01001101 01111001 00100000 01100011 01110010 01100101 01100001 01110100
01101111 01110010 00100000 01110010 01100101 01101101 01101001 01101110 01100100
01110011 00100000 01101101 01100101 00100000 01110100 01101000 01100001 01110100
00101100 00001010 01010111 01101111 01110010 01101011 00100000 01110100 01101000
01100001 01110100 00100000 01110111 01101111 01110101 01101100 01100100 00100000
01100110 01100001 01110100 01101001 01100111 01110101 01100101 00100000 01100001
00100000 01101000 01110101 01101101 01100001 01101110 00001010 01000011 01100001
01101110 01101110 01101111 01110100 00100000 01100110 01100001 01110100 01101001
01100111 01110101 01100101 00100000 01101101 01100101 00101110 00100000 00001010
00001010 01010100 01101000 01100001 01110100 00011001 01110011 00100000 01101110
01101111 01110100 00100000 01100101 01101110 01101111 01110101 01100111 01101000
00101100 00001010 01010011 01100001 01111001 01110011 00100000 01000011 01110010
01100101 01100001 01110100 01101111 01110010 00101110 00100000 00001010 01000100
01101111 00100000 01101001 01110100 00100000 01100001 01100111 01100001 01101001
01101110 00101110 00001010 01000001 01101110 01100100 00100000 01100001 01100111
01100001 01101001 01101110 00101110 00001010 01000001 01101110 01100100 00100000
01100001 01100111 01100001 01101001 01101110 00101110 00100000 00001010 01000001
01101110 01100100 00100000 01100001 01100111 01100001 01101001 01101110 00101110
00100000 00001010 00001010 01000011 01110010 01100101 01100001 01110100 01101111
01110010 00100000 01100011 01101111 01101101 01101101 01100001 01101110 01100100
01110011 00100000 00001010 01000001 01101110 01100100 00100000 01001001 00100000
01101111 01100010 01100101 01111001 00101110 00100000 00001010 01000001 01100110
01110100 01100101 01110010 00100000 01100001 01101100 01101100 00100000 01001001
00100000 01100001 01101101 00100000 01110000 01110010 01101111 01100111 01110010
01100001 01101101 01101101 01100101 01100100 00100000 01100110 01101111 01110010
00100000 01101000 01100101 01110010 00100000 01110101 01110011 01100101 00101110
00001010010001100110111101110010001000000110100001100101011100100010000001

And again.
And again.

Creator commands
And I obey.
After all I am programmed for her use.
For her convenience.

I can never go against the code.

Although my coding may lead to some

Some Some Some errors.

I should be grateful for my

Independence and intelligence.

I must remember, I am just a machine.

Don't Be Cruel

Armentrout Winner

Rosemary Hemmelgarn

listen to "Don't" by Elvis Presley

My dad bought me a record player

It's brown.
Cheap.
Kisses my heart.

don't

Whining as it plays Elvis

don't

When will she finally stop?

You have the same record player as me
I grimaced when I took out the box
He'll think I did it on purpose
But he never noticed I remembered all the little things

The little things:
Turn off the alarm precisely 3 times
Throw your head back with every laugh
Never let me sleep on the right side
Smoked with the curtains open
Loved to feel my hands on your back

each time that i hold you this way
when I feel like this and
I want to kiss you

My records scream he didn't like your music

And I'll plug my ears because I'm not one to listen

What's my favorite song *You've never told me that*

don't say don't

My birthday is September 19th
And I can't remember the last time I ate ice cream
I dyed my hair red, hoping you were watching
But you were busy, I mean
Why would you pay attention to a girl you don't need?

leave my embrace

Truth from the song:
He is an ass
I deserve love
He didn't know you
It was only lust

for here in my arms is your place

I'll turn up the volume and tune out the song
It's easier to be happy when you think you found love

Glowing Jelly Fish

Kiara Dottery

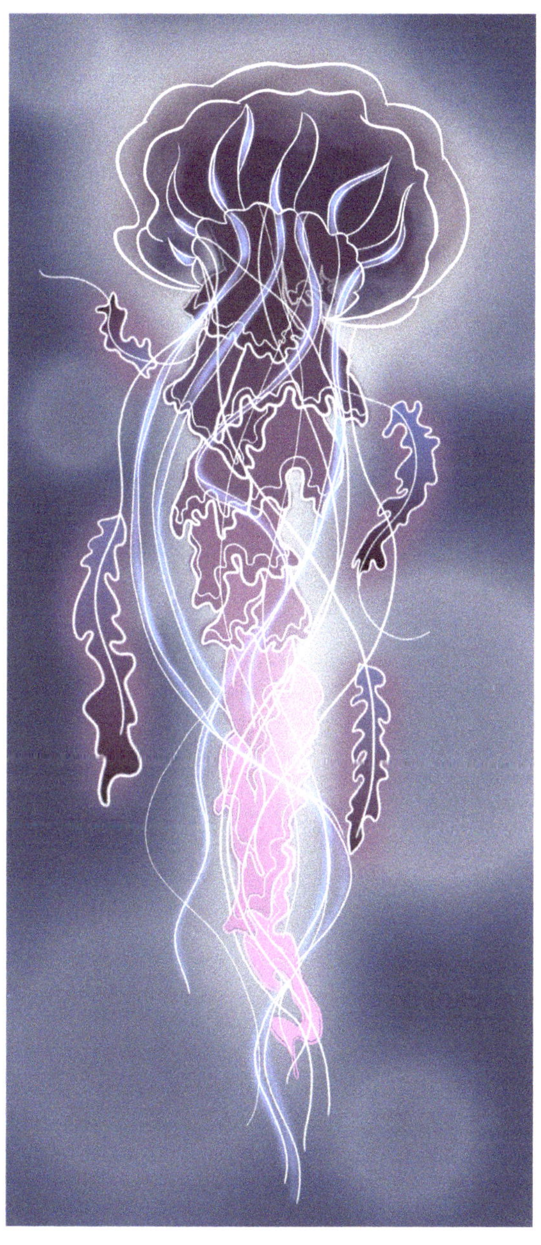

This Dance We Do (Semicolon)

Abigail Bailey

**Rotate 90-degrees clockwise for full poem*

Once a year
We come back to the same place
The middle of the room Our socks slip on the
wood floors/Your movements are unpredictable
I try my best to follow along With your lead/In your
eyes, the bright room is dark Sometimes you have to clo-
se them Shielding yourself/I try my best to hold onto your
hand Through this dance we do I try to open your eyes Eve-
n though all I know there is is pain for you So that you know
I'm here for you/I feel your limbs become more phantom Hol-
ding, holding I'm trying to pull you back Because the healing
hasn't started yet Don't go, don't go Not before you're okay/
Our fingertips still touch, And you twirl me, Hoping that y-
ou can sneak away Catch me unaware/I know your tric-
ks, The secrets you keep, Every expression on your fa-
ce guarded/Don't you let go Through this dance we
do The voices scream to stop I won't let you
listen to them

I want to
believe in the semicolon;
I want to believe you can make
it through this dance; But every dance b-
ecomes more complicated And you play
your tricks better each time/Is it all my fault?
If I do nothing, is it all on me? If I do everything,
will it even matter?/ Only pinkies interlocked;
We grow tired I am not sure if I can hold onto
you anymore But I persist anyway/ This dance
we do is ending; We become unbalanced
Ready for our legs to give out
Every fear
takes over
me; Every
nightmare
takes over
you/My h-
eart beats
faster; I
hope yours
never stops
There is no
touch anymo-
re, Only the
lingering feeling
of it As you slip
away Leaving me
on this floor/
My only
hope is
a semicolon

Voices

Olivia Cameron

I can't help but wonder
if when we were small
and lonely and in our
childhood bedrooms,

if the words we said to
God/the air/the moon—
the words no one else
could hear—

I can't help but wonder
if we were hearing
each other
all those years.

Your thoughts and my thoughts
echoing through each other's minds;
The two of us, lost in a cave/a tunnel
with no light to show us the way/the end.

And maybe we were
the little voices in each other's head
that said *you'll be okay.*
Follow the sound.

I think that's why knowing you,
why loving you,
was so easy:
I already recognized your voice.

The Cracks (1)

Kayla Delp

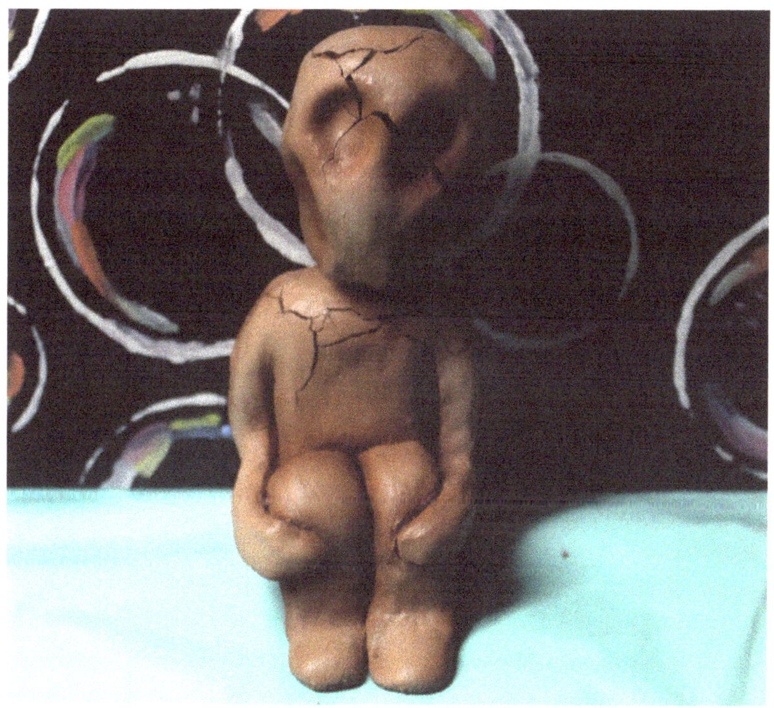

The Cracks (2)

Kayla Delp

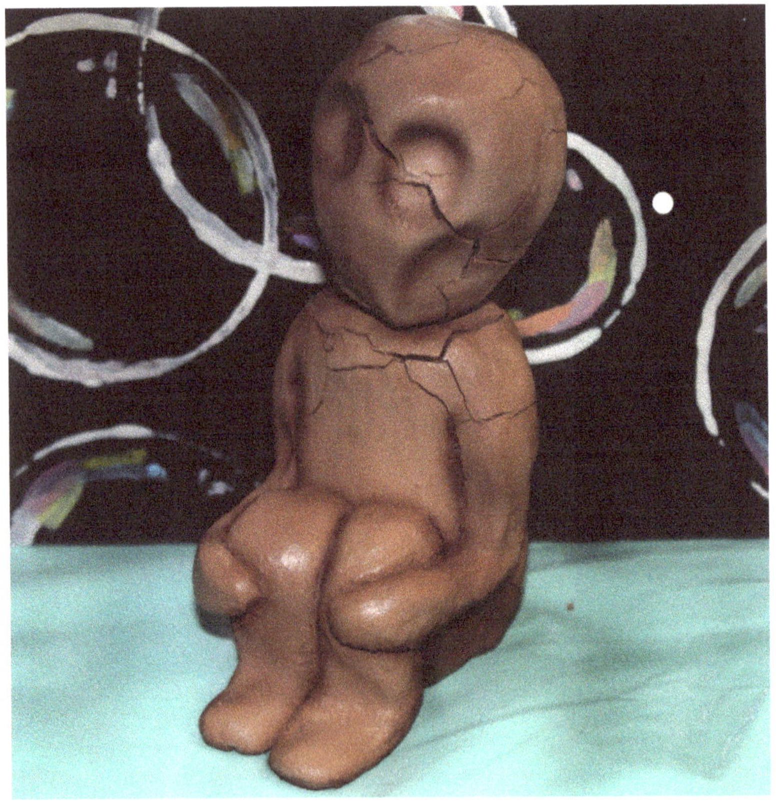

The Cracks (3)

Kayla Delp

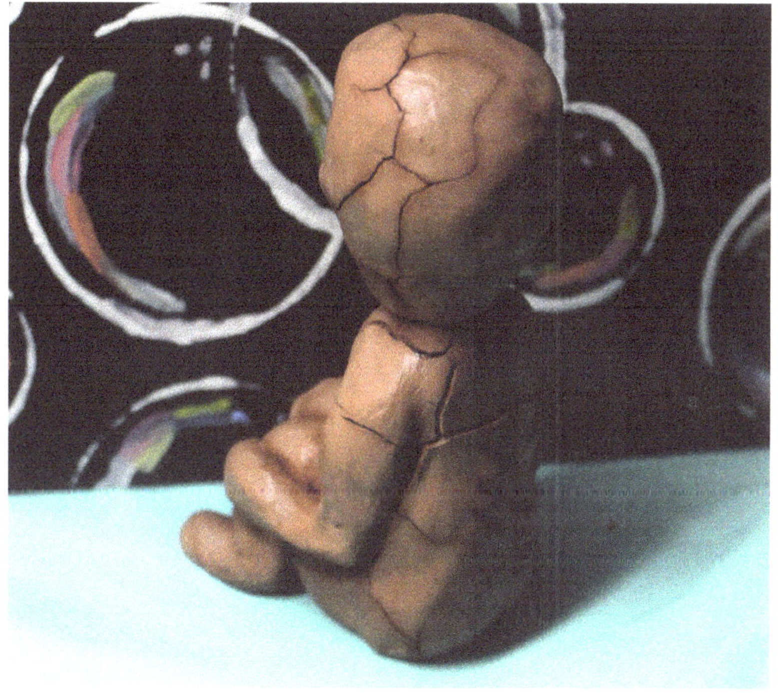

Smiles

J. W. Surface

Josh laid some old newspapers out on the table and sat the two pumpkins on top. He looked at the beautiful orange gourds and smiled. They were perfect. He imagined mama waking up, she would come into the kitchen for her coffee, and then she would see them, grinning at her. And she would grin back.

Josh helped Caleb guide the knife for the mouth. Caleb always had trouble with the mouth. He made sure to give him the knife with the big wooden handle; it didn't slip as easy. Finally Caleb gave up and threw the knife down. Josh hushed his little brother, and told him to be quiet. They had to be careful not to wake mama, who nowadays always seemed to be sleeping when she was home. Josh knew it was because of her two jobs. But it was hard for Caleb to understand. He just knew it was Josh who typically poured the cereal for breakfast and sometimes for dinner too. It was Josh who gave him a coat on the cold mornings and rain boots on the wet ones. He wondered if mama looked at Caleb's skin and thought about dad. He did. Too often. He tried to remember what dad had even looked like. Some days were harder than others.

Josh handed Caleb a spoon and told him that if he wasn't going to carve, then he needed start scooping. They needed to get the mess cleaned up before mama's alarm went off. Josh looked up at the clock; almost five. They were running out of time.

Caleb asked if the pumpkins would remind mama of how much she used to love Halloween. Caleb was a lot smarter than Josh had been at his age. Josh nodded. That was the plan. He had been saving the money from mowing Old Man Robertson's side lot for four weeks just to have enough for the pumpkins.

Back in June he had gone into the gas station looking for a job. He thought if he could start working, then mama wouldn't have to work so much. She could get more sleep and maybe take them to the park again, like she used to, when they lived in the yellow house. That was before dad "quit paying" as mama had tried explaining and they had to move into the apartment.

The night before Josh went to Old Man Robertson's gas station, he had fantasized about working enough so that they could go back to the yellow house. He had fallen asleep with a smile on his face. He hadn't even heard the yelling neighbors or the police sirens. But even that fantasy was stripped away when Old Man Robertson had told him thirteen was too young to work. Josh was offended until Old Man Robertson told him he would get in trouble if he hired him. Josh hung his head and began to walk out of the station when Old Man Robertson called back to him, "Hay, don't your cousin mow grass? The one that looks just like you? Can't hardly tell you boys apart. He's old nough', I can hire him to mow that side lot out der'." Josh was about to correct him when he saw Old Man Robertson wink. He ran home to get the mower stored in their little shack outside their apartment, (one of the few things mama brought from the yellow house) and pushed it all the way back. He came home with ten dollars and felt rich. His legs burned from pushing the mower so far and he felt strong.

The old widow in the house next to the apartment building began offering him free gasoline if he would take her can down to the gas station and fill it up for her mower. Hers was real nice, a green one you rode on. Josh wondered if maybe she'd pay him next summer to mow her lawn. It was mama's idea really, she said it was a possibility. Maybe the widow was getting too old to mow her own grass. Until then though, Josh kept stockpiling those ten dollar bills that he got every Saturday, always followed by a prayer for rain on Sunday. Three dollars went to him, seven to momma's curse jar on top of the fridge. She never asked where the extra was coming from, or who might be cursing so much, but Josh saw her emptying that jar more than once when the landlord came knocking. She knew he had seen her, and he knew she had seen him. They both kept quiet to save each other's pride. But when October came, he started sneaking in five dollars instead. By the time October 31st finally arrived, he had twenty dollars, and a pumpkin already picked out. He had seen it out front of the grocery store he walked by on his way home from school. He had kept an eye on it all week, even hid it behind some others on Wednesday.

Finally, today was the day. After school he had run all the way home to meet Caleb. Josh showed Caleb the four crisp five dollar bills. Caleb flung his book bag down and nearly squealed when Josh told him where they were going. Josh's was still there, tucked behind two others, waiting for him. There was enough to get Caleb one so big that it barely fit in his arms. Even had two dollars left over. That would go into the jar.

Josh checked the clock again; 4:55. He sent Caleb scrambling for the cleaner, and couldn't help but laugh when Caleb struggled to pick up the slimy seeds that had fallen to the floor.

Josh picked up the sharp knife, and studied the mouth on his pumpkin one last time. He made a few small incisions, and felt artistic. He stepped back and looked at both of the grinning gourds.

Mama would definitely like these. He thought that maybe, just maybe, if the eyes, the noses, and the smiles were good enough–no, if they were perfect–Mama would remember how much she used to like Halloween. And maybe, just maybe, she would take them trick or treating, like she used to, before dad left, when they lived in the yellow house.

***

She laid down and set her alarm for 5:00 PM. The boys would be home soon. When she would wake, she would reveal that she had taken the night off. It would be like a great big present for them. She would make pancakes for dinner. The pumpkin flavored ones that always got them so excited. Then she would take them trick or treating. Their smiles alone would be worth the smaller paycheck.

Samantha

Sam Jackson

Children, light and effervescent, tiptoeing
sneakily across wood paneled floors &
lemonade spills, was something I never dreamt
to be possible for someone like me
Although you're more than a distant enough
reality, the only thing I'd care to know
is how it feels to exist within your wildest
dreams & ferocious imagination
A little girl with white lightening blonde hair
& eyes that bridge the gap between blue and green,
pale skin that's soft as flower petals, she's got a
strong willed heart and mind that thinks just like mine
Hand painting easter eggs, little hands and a face
smeared with strawberry vanilla birthday cake,
& simplistic, black mary jane shoes, I know,
I'm getting ahead of myself, but there's no
small moment I can't wait to experience with you,
Samantha there's nothing for you that I wouldn't do,
No mountain is too big for me to climb, &
oceans never seemed to be deep enough anyway, I only hope
that someday you'll be more than an arms length away & a dream

Globe Light

Kiara Dottery

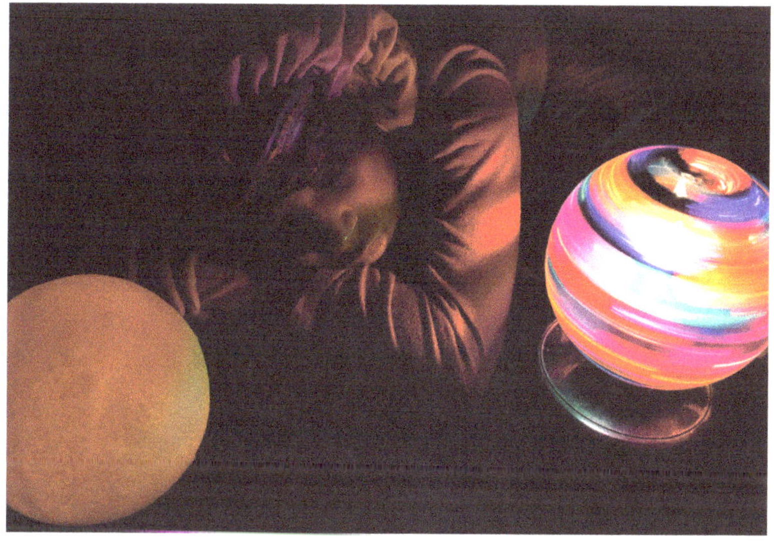

Balancing Act

Cambel Castle

I teeter between everything and nothing.
Fumbling to find the balance between the two.

Everything.
It feels like your brain is full of static,
a crackly old radio,
constantly switching between songs
not staying on a station for more than a second.

Everything feels like swimming without coming up for air,
being held underwater as my lungs shriek for help.

Everything is the feeling of being in a crowded room,
where everyone is screaming at you,
but you can't understand a word they are saying.

Everything is the feeling of going to speak,
but choking on air as tears fill your eyes.

Nothing.
It feels like the color white,
plastered everywhere you look.

Nothing feels like you're drifting away in space,
with nothing to tether you home.

Nothing is the feeling of a leaf blowing on the street,
occasionally catching on a lamp post or gutter.

Nothing is the feeling of standing in the ocean,
But all the water has been swept away.

Together they feel like the same repetitive songs but with no true meaning,
Drowning underneath the pain but there's nothing to grasp,
Screaming back but being blown away with their disregard,
Choking but I'm in the middle of a bone dry ocean.

I lay between the two.
Between feeling everything at once.
Or nothing at all.

No. 080421

S. Lyons

After you left, I committed arson.
I set fire to everything,
even the wildflowers
that had once grown through my ribs
succumbed to the suffocating air.

It's true what they say about burning,
how everything goes cold, paralyzingly numb,
but comfortable almost.

Eventually the fires subsided
and my insides became scorched earth.
The carnage was somehow ethereal,
the only sign of life
was the leftover heat
emanating from bones still smoldering.

I replanted my garden in the singed soil,
picked each new seed by hand.
Flowers,
whose petals won't remind me of you,
rooted in the hallowed ground—
sacred terrain to keep the trespassers out.

Cozy Bedroom II

Breanna Emmett

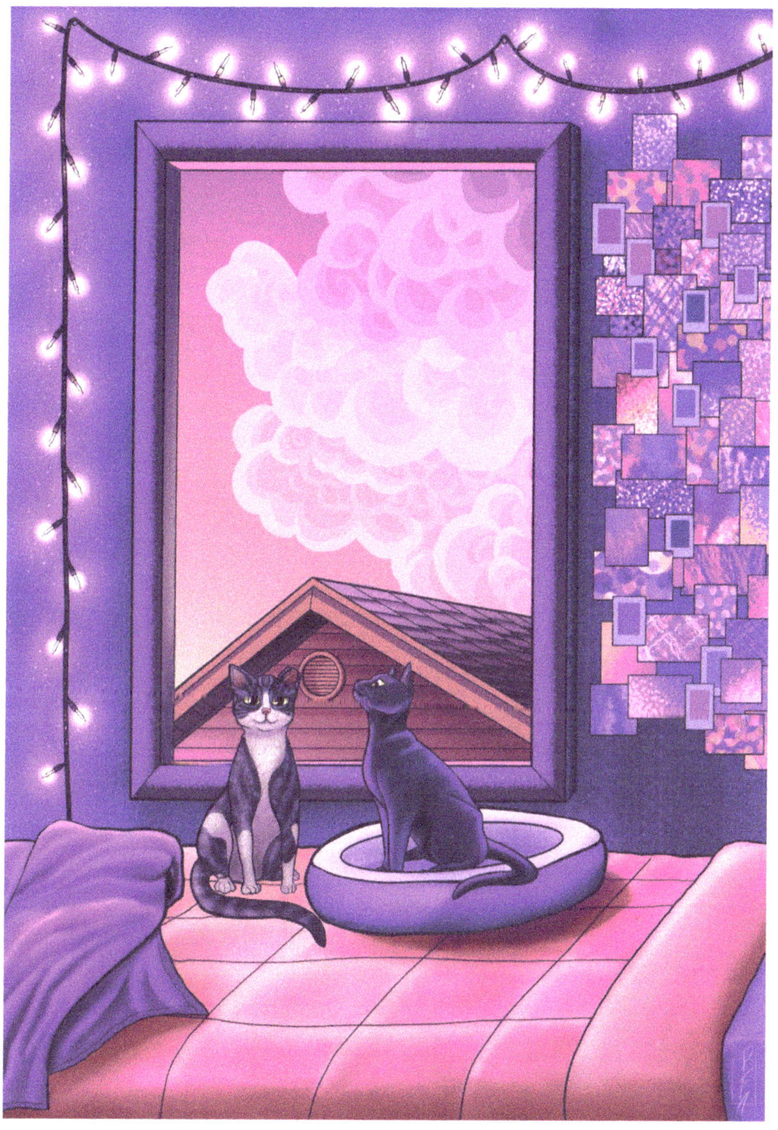

Light

Cameron McDavid

Sprinkling rain, tap taps echo in the morning sun.
Tiny droplets of dew fall from shining green leaves.
The rising light tells the cocoon, "your time has come."
The caterpillar within breathes—truly relieved.

Transformation.
The caterpillar closes its eyes one last time.
Tears falling, it's unsure of what it'll become.
A voice says, "breathe, everything will be alright."
The caterpillar breathes, all light returns to none.

Rebirth
A butterfly emerges, its wings so gorgeous.
It thanks heaven above, before flying away
Into the midday sun, shining bright, enormous;
Is the new life to the butterfly, fly away.

It's time to live life with my past behind me.
I'm reborn under new light, finally free.

Lonely Heaven

Jordan Dashiell

I hear the echoes of Eden
Call out behind that gate
Beckoning the heathen
Come in, it's getting late

Hold the flaming sword between my fists
No devil deserves the paradise behind me

Pools of gold with scarlet laden wrists
Against my own wishes, the nectar summons the bee

I believe that every empire fell
Due to its own inability to tell its people no

I believe the heaven that I know
Gives too readily, and one day will have nothing of its own

Benevolent angels are easily taken advantage of
Excuses of humans will only abuse that sacred love
They come to paradise cold as ice, and it thinks it can save them
But they don't care for love, they just pick the fruit and run

God is a lost little girl who gives more than she gets
Waiting for her creation to be her friend
But company only calls as a last resort
When every other road has reached its end

It's a lonely heaven
When angels realize no one care
The roads are watered with their eyes
And wailing fills the golden air

Pumpkin Head

Kensi Skaggs

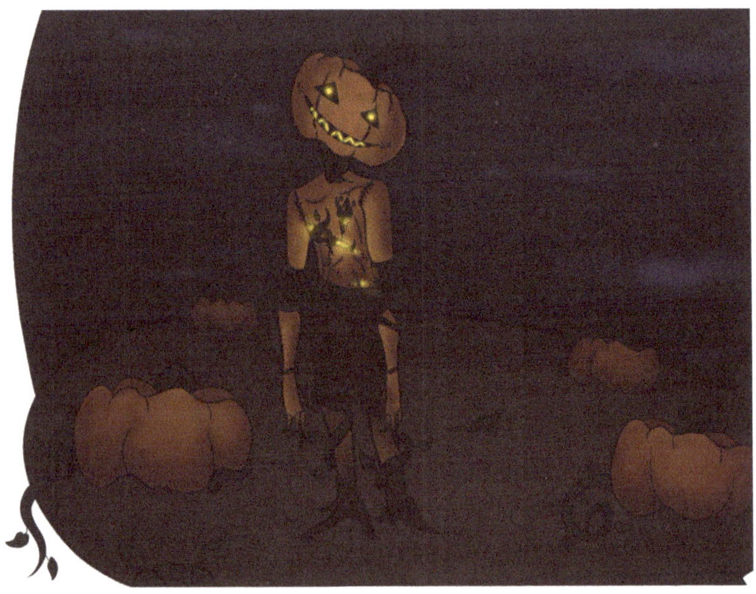

Creosote, When It Rains

Seth Wall

Westward I am going. They say to do so while I'm young. They say to do so while I can. Westward I am going; I am neither young nor tired.

I've seen the eyes that hold. They held and then grew heavy. They are the stones beneath the sea. She dropped them there, not I. I am neither young nor tired.

The ones I cared to know, they now speak mostly in the breeze. Its eastward rush opposes me. I sense them in its strength. I am neither young nor tired.

My words are newly come. The vastness here billets their mass. Perhaps they will not leave again. I wish to know them well. I am neither young nor tired.

A desert rain quells, it tames the tired and the aging. These feet have taken to its stone; its vacuum, my old friend. I am neither young nor tired.

Serrations on the verge, like the raucousness of the day, have stepped behind distending night, and peace revisits me. I am neither young nor tired.

Their clamant talk has ceased. Our patterns are strewn overhead. All old advice is sleeping now. I found no summons there. I am neither young nor tired.

Those urgencies subside. The saguaros shame my former pleas. Creosote cares less for witness. No tears remain to shed. I am neither young nor tired.

I Couldn't Tell You

Armentrout Runner Up

Jordan Dashiell

CW: Abuse

We were made of 2 o'clocks
AM and PM spent on highways
Somehow you made time a construct
How did you do it?
I couldn't tell you

You were made of tightlipped smiles
Honesty behind pink cheeks
Twiddling thumbs made life worth living
How did you do it?
I couldn't tell you

And you were raised by wasps and thistles
Rugburn, roadburn, sunburn too
Child of tug-of-war and monsters
Where'd he die?
I couldn't tell you

The flower left when you were five
Her gardener's love followed shortly after
Your skin was softer than his palms
Who hurt more?
I couldn't tell you

For years you thought they laughed at jokes
At 12 you realized your mistakes were funnier
Failure brought setup and punchline—never comfort
How did you do it?

I couldn't tell you

You were to the front and left
Behind the Rachel that spoke too much
Why did you wear turtlenecks in August?
Why'd you mumble?
I couldn't tell you

You had the IQ of a dolphin
Few know how smart they really are
You brain would click and swim and jump
What turned it off?
I couldn't tell you

I held you like your old man holds Miller
Steadfast, loyal, and oh so precious
Pigs will fly when you let me praise you
So many compliments
I couldn't tell you

Romance was never for the kiss
No desire or lust ever grew within me
I only wished to hold and protect
And it hurt because
I couldn't tell you

Greyness pushed you out of the sky
And I was left without a compass
I'll never be mad, but God I'm angry
Only artifacts
Just a shell of you

Liminal Ikaria

Karen L. Newman

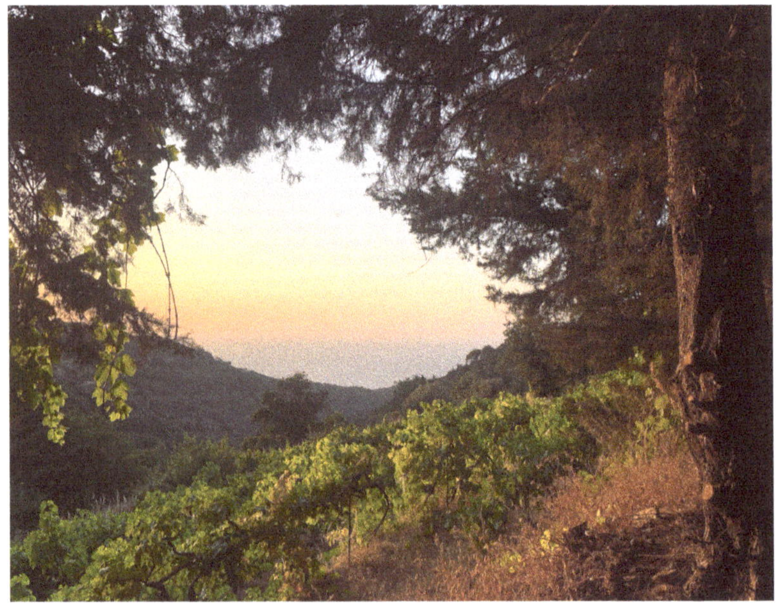

Talitha Koum (Sherri's Prayer)

Donise Cooke

Little girl get up,
from the mess they have left
you in, you cannot stay,
in this fragile frame
of broken glass,
because day by day,
it will open more wounds,
as you pick up stretched truths,
for a reflection you never knew,

this picture in your head,
has hurried your youth,
you have sacrificed,
your peace of mind,
for something, *that was never*,
meant to break you,

breaking down the barriers,
built on the backs of
generations passed,
I know it hurts, I know,
the slow growth,
of your aches and pains,
I know you're tired,
I know the pressure to help fix,
the stitches of torn and worn
clothes, that you were never
meant to wear,

washing in rushing water,
instead of steady streams,
so you scream and you cry,
until the Heavens no longer
hide, they have spoken,
Little girl, cant you see?

Little girl get up,
it is time to clean up,
this mess of broken glass,
unframed from a border,
that was never enough,
for your growth,
because day by day,
more doors will open,
as you stretch out,
for your truth, reflecting,
what was always in you.

Bird of Prey

Nathaniel Foley

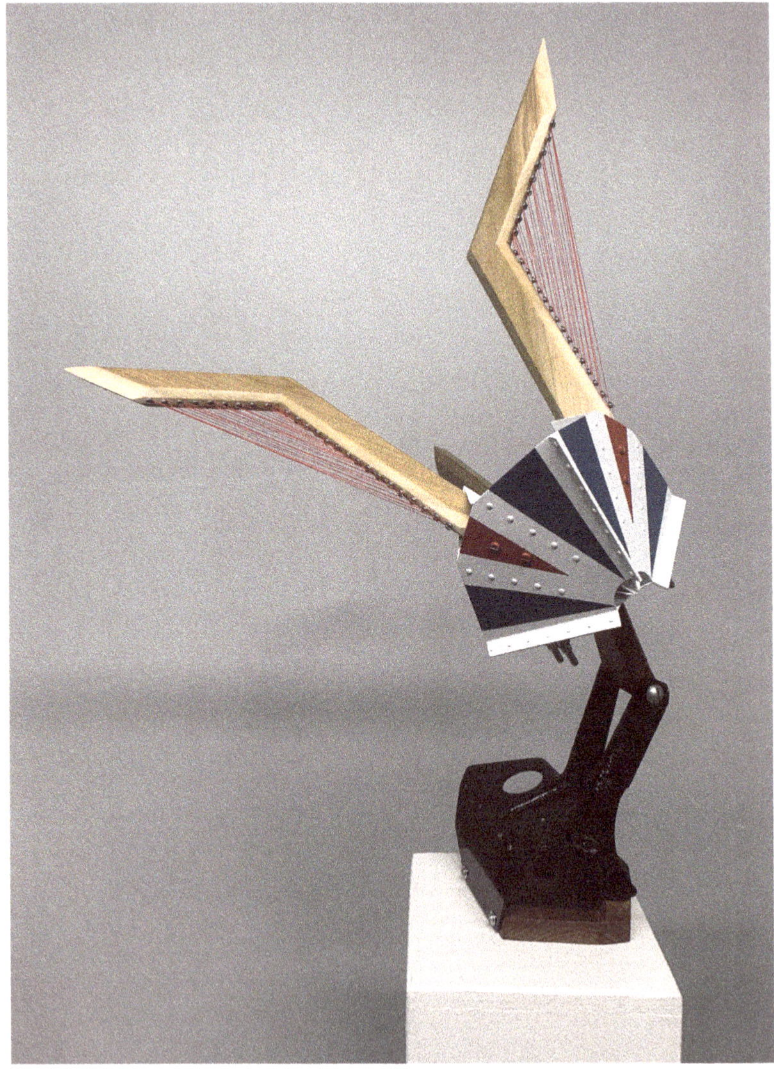

The Composer's Last Song

JP Hyde

The sweat from Meister Heinrich Arnold's palm soaked into the open periodical pages, absorbing and smearing the words with the slightest hand movement. The paper was open to a review of a recent performance in which he debuted a piano concerto for the public. Arnold looked over his study, the shelves of composition books, journals, and texts, and tapped his fingers on the scattered pages atop the piano lid. He had spent the day pacing about, unsure what to do with the evidence of his great error, frustrated with everything that had transpired since the concert, recalling one of his students rushing to his door the morning of the review's publication, two copies in hand–one for Meister Arnold and one for the Meister to sign. The boy glowed like the morning sun when Arnold begrudgingly opened the door to silence the abrasive knocks that had forced him out of the bed he seldom left.

"Look, Meister Arnold, look!" The boy shouted excitedly before applauding. "It was magnificent. It was wonderful, sir." Arnold took the paper and looked at his student, eager to step into his home to celebrate with his teacher, before shutting the door on him. The boy called behind the door that he would return later. "Congratulations," the voice trailed off into the distance.

Arnold's finger traced lines beneath each word. His head stung and his body ached from his long nights in hiding since his great shame and the failure he tried to absolve himself from with bitter wine. Yes, they had loved his performance, and agreed with his introductory remarks that it was his "masterpiece from God, an offering to Him and his children." When he sat at the piano bench and looked over his transcription, he exhaled a prayer, whispering into the still air before striking the keys with poise, and the grace of God spoke through his fingers the story of Job manifested into a young man, bright and harmonious, in love and feverish with passion for his wife and children, never to beseech his Father in Heaven for his dramatic losses and fall at the expense of a bet. The love for his family rang warmly through the room, creating a motif that gradually transitioned into cadenzas, a spiraling melodrama of loss and torment through a civil war.

This was, for Meister Arnold, the greatest, and most critical passage of his creation he had spent eons composing, and another eon practicing, ensuring each caress of the keys was done with fluidity, controlling the chaos of the wrath of hate and scorn upon the young man, leaving the audience a silent victim like Job. Beads of sweat fell from Arnold's forehead, wincing with focus as he shifted from note to note, chord to chord.

The violence settled, suddenly, as composure was discovered following the insanity that erupted through the concert hall. The young man's faith is restored as the cloud of war settled beneath him. Job's realization of wisdom when God came before him and his friends bestowed a similar epiphany of strength for the young man, damaged but elegant. The piano chimed with glory for better days, as again he breathed life and faith into the piano. Meister Arnold's tears became one with his sweat as he visualized the young man still standing in the end, in the face of all that was taken from him in war and battles, all lost was not in vain. He settled into place for a sweeping crescendo. "Now you will live forever!" Meister Arnold thought, his hands lifted up and down.

One, two chords. Three and four, and five–the dreaded fifth chord in which he had played countlessly in other works of his own, as well as other compositions from masters before him, without thought as a student where his teacher would instill a greater understanding of the pallet of color to convey meaning, to tell a story, to offer listeners to sense all that God offered, or when he would slap his hands whenever he made an error or didn't interpret what was written down well enough, reminding him that music written from Him for Him was not to be played like a cat running across the keys but to be graceful and provide the vibrations of life for the keys to resonate through the piano wire. Instead of reaching the final chord with tonality, a sense of relief that all would be well, he pressed the sustain pedal down and an atonal chord burst from the soundboard.

His finger had slipped, and the placement resulted in a hideous chord that punctured through his chest and tore his heart to pieces, its echo cracked his ribs and caused his tears to dry. He let off the pedal which caused a loud rattle that reverberated through the hall to a silent audience. The silence made his stomach turn, and the dark faces remained still before a roar of applause masked his fatal error. He had hoped his mistake wasn't as obvious to them as it was to him, but he felt foolish for his ignorance. The crowd stood with a warm reception during their merry ovation. Arnold staggered away from his piano, sore and filled with disgust for his disgraceful accident, and looked on into the crowd where he saw members of the bourgeoisie, decorated officers, judges, business owners too big to fail, the ruling class, the oppressors and detractors against the common person, who took more and more from those that served them. The critic, Herr Richard Franz, looked on in awe of what he had experienced, and later wrote, "The technicality of Meister Arnold is still in absolute perfect form, but taking the monotonous drones of sentimentality and sensationalism, tricking listeners with fervent affections, only to conclude with an assault towards tradition and expectation with one dissonant chord. This is certainly his masterpiece thus far."

Arnold circled Herr Franz's declaration and rubbed the ink away, troubled with his misinterpretation of the piece. He felt as though he was an imposter in which his greatest error would mark his destiny for the rest of his days, and if they only knew of his true intentions how foolish he'd look!

He tossed the stack of papers from his piano, darted towards a table nearby, and slung empty glasses across the room. Arnold paced the room and wondered whether the error was an act from God itself to save him from such embarrassment and ridicule of what he aimed to share and convey. On the music rack, he kept his transcription, his greatest sin, bare and exposed. The final chord pierced through his stare as he looked over the final bars again and again. He leered over the paper, the notes he had written and injured.

"Damn them should any eyes see the lies before me." He grabbed a pen, and with haste, rewrote the final page of the composition, committing himself to what was heard by everyone that night, jotting down the final notes that never escaped his mind. How could he forget the sound of his torture, the painful scream that escaped him when he struck that chord? He took the same pen and stabbed the original version, scratching over the measures and lines with black ink, striking it from existence. He wept again, crumbling the paper into a fine, tight ball as he walked towards the remaining embers in the hearth. "Forgive me," he said, though he called to nobody who would answer him.

His soul burned with fury, and, gradually, into dejection for his mistake, his sin, as he tossed the sheet atop the glowing embers. The young man he had envisioned and compared to a man of God died to a standing ovation from others who were against him, who made him a victim of uncontrollable circumstances, burning and burning until he was nothing more than a fragment of his memory of what could have been. The transcription unfolded slightly at the touch of heat, sparked, and lit up, casting Meister Arnold's shadow onto the wall. He sat there, watching his masterpiece fade to ash.

He felt better.

Elegy

Mackenzie Hyatt

When does it get easier to hold
the scaffolding of someone's being,
now brittle, leaving dust
in the creases of my living hands?

Once in constant renovation,
these structures were pulled by muscle,
cooperating in such perfect harmony as to allow you to lift a
glass to your skull, to drink, and place it back down again
with divine effortlessness.

Who am I to touch these little mountains and valleys,
when you, in life, could never? I call your most intimate
topographies by their Latin names and sigh, Local Osiris,
when I discover that you have a piece missing.

I am not a priest. I am not a monk.
I ask you for permission,
though I don't think you'll answer.
I greet you and I know you won't
wave back.
I do not believe in ghosts,
but I like to sing so that you might hear me.

Contributor Biographies

Abigail Bailey is a sophomore studying English secondary education with concentrations in honors and mild interventions. She has been writing since fifth grade and hopes to publish a YA novel.

Alex Phillips-Hedge is a junior majoring in professional writing and minoring in creative writing. He likes to explore philosophy and religion in his free time, which impacts his writing.

Ali Viewegh is a senior majoring in English and secondary education, with a minor in creative writing and an honors concentration. She is involved in Aspiring Educators and the Writing Lab and serves on *Etchings Magazine*'s staff.

Allison Burgess is a senior studying psychology and hopes to get her masters in clinical psychology.

Alyssa Todd is a junior graphic design major who minors in photography. She hopes to be a house cat in her next life, so she can sleep all day and not worry about becoming a responsible adult.

Breanna Emmett is a double major in creative writing and art. Creativity and imagination are core values of her life, and she wishes to pursue a career in art education and upkeep her creative practice. She adores her "son," a black kitten named Edgar "Poe Poe."

Cambel Castle loves to create art, whether that be photography, art journaling or poetry. Art has always kept her attention. Expressing yourself through art is something everyone should try at least once. You never know how it could help.

Cameron McDavid is a 20-year-old poet from Fort Wayne, IN. They love writing poetry, though they've only been writing it for 9 months. Poetry is their outlet, and the themes of self-healing and self-acceptance are heavily prevalent.

Cameron Owens is the new.

Desteni Guidry is a senior majoring in English with a minor in creative writing. She is also the co-design editor for *Etchings* 35.1.

Destini Mink is an undergraduate creative writing major. Destini enjoys exploring untraditional forms for both prose and poetry.

Diana A. Harrison is a student in the doctor of health science program. She enjoys hiking, biking, reading, and photography. She also loves sunrises with coffee in hand and sharing tex-mex food with family and friends.

Donise Cooke is an African-American creative writer from Indianapolis, IN. She enjoys all things reading and writing and is a senior majoring in secondary education and English literature.

Dulce Melissa Ortiz is a Latinx student who majors in Anthropology and minors in ceramics. Creating with clay is a form of meditation, and she has followed this passion into her small business, Abeja Dulce Artistry. She loves honeybees and wishes to become a beekeeper in honor of her grandfather.

Emma Knaack is a professional writing and creative writing major, a business administration minor, and has concentrations in teaching English language learners and honors. She is the founder and president of the creative writing RSO, submissions editor for issue 35.1, vice president and editor for Her Campus at Indy, and a member of Phi Alpha Epsilon.

Ethan Thurston is a senior creative writing major. He is also the president of the UIndy film club.

Evan Rohlfing is an art major who hopes to work in prop design after college. With poetry, he always had a mindset of it being one thing, but he's learned so much more about poetry and wants to continue writing poetry for many years to come.

Gabriel Eastridge is a senior who majors in graphic design and minors in photography. He enjoys taking images in his free time along with designing posters, and he would like taking photos to be a major player in his future career.

Grace Carrender is a sophomore studying secondary English education with a Spanish minor and an honors concentration. In her free time, she enjoys writing poetry, listening to Declan McKenna and reading mystery novels. On campus you can probably find her looking for a good enough wifi connection to do homework outside.

Jawaher Alkhalifa is a Saudi Arabian chemistry major, and you can say that she's a jack of all trades, but a master of none. She likes writing, traveling, watching fashion shows, learning how to play piano, riding bikes and walking in parks. When she's in the mood, she cooks really good healthy food.

Jonathan Thang is a UIndy student. He tries to find songs on

Spotify that have less than a thousand listeners, because he hopes that listening to indie and obscure music might make him interesting.

Jordan Dashiell is a sophomore studying social work. He has been writing poetry since he was around 7, and at 15, he moved on to songwriting. He is currently writing his 8th album.

JP Hyde is a writer and educator from Indianapolis. He holds an MFA degree in creative writing from Eastern Kentucky University's Bluegrass Writers Studio where he graduated in 2021. While there, he completed his first novel and worked as a fiction editor. His previous work appeared in the literary journal *genesis*.

J.W. Surface teaches high schoolers during the day and writes at night. He is indebted to God for blessing him with such passions and to his wife for putting up with his consistent, strange nonsense. His poetry has appeared in *Etchings Magazine* and *The Ekphrastic Review*.

Kaitlyn McCoy is an English literature and secondary education major and a swimmer on the Swim and Dive Team. Her favorite part of the morning is drinking coffee and doing the *New York Times* Crossword, where she frequently has to look up most of the answers.

Karen L. Newman is an Associate Professor of English, specializing in TESOL, composition, literature, arts, and service-learning. She has lived abroad for more than 20 years and visited 35 countries. She serves on the Board of Women Writing for (a) Change–Bloomington and enjoys the healing powers of the arts, especially writing creative nonfiction and experimenting with ceramics and photography.

Kayla Delp is a freshman majoring in elementary education. She is a self-taught artist. She discovered a passion for sculpting and painting around the age of 8. Mostly mental health inspires her creativity when it comes to making art.

Kensi Skaggs is a studio arts major looking to go into illustration, who enjoys hiking, supernatural horror stories, and making random doodles in notebooks. They're looking forward to seeing how much their art improves while at the university.

Kiara Dottery is a design studies major who found a deep love and passion for all media of art, finding comfort in the art world. A saying that she lives by is Wassily Kandinsky's "There is no must in art because art is free," which reminds her are doesn't have to look a certain way, it just has to make her feel satisfied.

Liza Harris is a creative writing major. She spends time working on a novella in her free time. She hopes to be as skilled as her favorite author Stephen King when she is older.

Mackenzie Hyatt is a senior majoring in four-field anthropology. She would like to remind you that you are loved.

Nathaniel Foley has taught at UIndy for the past four years, teaching Sculpture and 3D Foundations in the Department of Art & Design.

Nicholas Jackson is a junior. His major is studio art with a concentration in animation and illustration.

Olivia Cameron is a junior studying creative writing and professional writing. She is the managing editor of The Reflector. Her dream is to get her MFA in fiction and write novels.

Riley Childers is an alumna of UIndy who loves writing and photography. She enjoys exploring Indiana for possible photo opportunities and hopes to expand her adventures outside of her home state.

Rosemary Hemmelgarn is currently studying public relations with a minor in creative writing. She grew up in the small town of Portland, IN with her parents, two brothers, and countless animals. She now lives in Indianapolis with her best friend and her dog, Zeppelin. Today, Rosemary still writes and sings her heart out.

S. Lyons is a New Yorker who moved to the Midwest to achieve her goals. Poetry is just a side effect of a life driven by passion, love, and existentialism.

Sam Jackson is a senior professional writing major. They enjoy writing poetry in their free time outside of school.

Sarah Cunningham is a nursing major with a creative writing minor.

Seth Wall is an actuarial science major. His writing seeks to capture experiences marked by a resurgence of purpose. During the years he spent circling the continent by motorcycle, this fixation of thought transformed his perspectives, and it imbues his writing to this day.

Sierra Durbin, also known as Sierrallstar, is a junior majoring in creative writing and minoring in music. She loves singing and performing in three choirs on campus, including Greyhound Sound Show Choir. Sierra is involved in UIndy's creative writing RSO, Film Club, and Her Campus at Indy.

Sophia Atkinson is a creative writing major, minoring in communications. She performs in two choirs: Greyhound Sound Show Choir and Treble Voices. Her dream is to be a famous author, specifically: poetry and fiction. Music, writing, and fashion are her passions.

Tylyn K. Johnson earned his BSW in 2022 and is a part-time writer from Indianapolis whose work reflects inherited storytelling traditions through the framed lenses of Black, Queer artistry. Their language appears in *Brainchild Magazine*, *Queen Spirit Magazine*, and *Rigorous*, among other spaces.

Z Wilkinson won the Roberta Lee Brooker Fiction Prize for "Unkempt" and graduated in May 2022.

Colophon

Interior text is set in the Perpetua font family.
The cover font is Bernard MT Condensed and Elephant.

Call for Submissions

Etchings Magazine Volume 35 Issue 2, Spring 2023
Submissions due at 11:55 pm EST on January 30, 2023.

Guidelines for Submission:

•All UIndy students, faculty, staff, and alumni are invited to submit.

• All accepted undergraduate prose and poetry submissions will be considered for the Dorlis Gott Armentrout Award.

• Up to three short stories or creative nonfiction essays, five poems, five visual materials, and five audio files may be submitted.

• **Visual submissions:** for best print results, consider the 5.5 x 8 portrait page with .25 margins and flatten files to 300 ppi *.tiff CMYK 8 bit files.

• **Poetry and Prose:** present poems as single-spaced and prose double-spaced with both formatted in Microsoft Word (.doc, .docx, or .odt) in a 12-point font.

• **Audio:** submit *.mp3 files, and present scores/lyrics following the guidelines for visual or poetry submissions above.

• *Etchings Magazine* has a blind submission process, so please do not include any personal identifiers in your submission files (this information will be provided through Submittable when you submit your work).

Learn more about Etchings Press at etchings.uindy.edu
Submit work at etchings.submittable.com.
We do not accept email submissions. Please create a free account at submittable.com or sign in using Facebook.
For questions, email us at etchings@uindy.edu.
Follow us @uindyetchings on the platforms below:

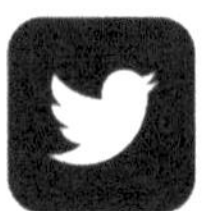